WITHDRAWN

The Terrorism Problem

ISSUES

Volume 147

Series Editor

Lisa Firth

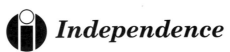

Independence

Educational Publishers
Cambridge

First published by Independence
The Studio, High Green
Great Shelford
Cambridge CB22 5EG
England

© Independence 2008

British Library Cataloguing in Publication Data

The Terrorism Problem – (Issues Series)
I. Firth, Lisa II. Series
303.6'25

ISBN 978 1 86168 420 2

Printed in Great Britain

MWL Print Group Ltd

Cover

The illustration on the front cover is by
Angelo Madrid.

CONTENTS

Chapter One: Terrorism

Chapter Two: Tackling Terrorism

Useful information for readers

Dear Reader,

Issues: The Terrorism Problem

The issue of international terrorism is difficult to ignore, confronting us daily in the media and dominating the political landscape. Many people fear its ability to impact on their lives, with one in seven UK adults fearful of having children due to the threat of terrorism. This book looks at what kinds of terrorism exist and why, at the impacts of terrorism, current trends in political violence and at the media focus on terrorism – does this help or hinder counter-terrorist measures?

The purpose of Issues

The Terrorism Problem is the one hundred and forty-seventh volume in the **Issues** series. The aim of this series is to offer up-to-date information about important issues in our world. Whether you are a regular reader or new to the series, we do hope you find this book a useful overview of the many and complex issues involved in the topic.

Titles in the **Issues** series are resource books designed to be of especial use to those undertaking project work or requiring an overview of facts, opinions and information on a particular subject, particularly as a prelude to undertaking their own research.

The information in this book is not from a single author, publication or organisation; the value of this unique series lies in the fact that it presents information from a wide variety of sources, including:

⇨ Government reports and statistics
⇨ Newspaper articles and features
⇨ Information from think-tanks and policy institutes
⇨ Magazine features and surveys
⇨ Website material
⇨ Literature from lobby groups and charitable organisations.*

Critical evaluation

Because the information reprinted here is from a number of different sources, readers should bear in mind the origin of the text and whether the source is likely to have a particular bias or agenda when presenting information (just as they would if undertaking their own research). It is hoped that, as you read about the many aspects of the issues explored in this book, you will critically evaluate the information presented. It is important that you decide whether you are being presented with facts or opinions. Does the writer give a biased or an unbiased report? If an opinion is being expressed, do you agree with the writer?

The Terrorism Problem offers a useful starting point for those who need convenient access to information about the many issues involved. However, it is only a starting point. Following each article is a URL to the relevant organisation's website, which you may wish to visit for further information.

Kind regards,

Lisa Firth
Editor, **Issues** series

*Please note that Independence Publishers has no political affiliations or opinions on the topics covered in the **Issues** series, and any views quoted in this book are not necessarily those of the publisher or its staff.*

ISSUES TODAY
A RESOURCE FOR KEY STAGE 3

Younger readers can also now benefit from the thorough editorial process which characterises the **Issues** series with the launch of a new range of titles for 11- to 14-year-old students, **Issues Today**. In addition to containing information from a wide range of sources, rewritten with this age group in mind, **Issues Today** titles also feature comprehensive glossaries, an accessible and attractive layout and handy tasks and assignments which can be used in class, for homework or as a revision aid. In addition, these titles are fully photocopiable. For more information, please visit the **Issues Today** section of our website (www.independence.co.uk).

Classifying terrorism

Key facts from the US Foreign Policy Association

Defining terrorism

There is no globally accepted definition of terrorism. Most scholarly texts devoted to the study of terrorism contain a section, chapter, or chapters devoted to a discussion of how difficult it is to define the term. In fact, various US government agencies employ different definitions of the term. The most widely accepted definition is probably that put forward by the US State Department, which defines terrorism as 'premeditated, politically motivated violence perpetrated against noncombatant targets by subnational groups or clandestine agents, usually intended to influence an audience' [Title 22 of the United States Code, Section 2656f(d)].

Etymology

The word 'terrorism' was coined during France's Reign of Terror in 1793-94. Originally, the leaders of this systematised attempt to weed out 'traitors' among the revolutionary forces praised terror as the best way to defend liberty, but as the Revolution progressed, the word soon came to be associated with state violence and the guillotine. Today, most terrorists eschew the label, preferring to perceive themselves as irregular military forces [e.g. Irish Republican Army (IRA), Revolutionary Armed Forces of Colombia (FARC), Symbionese Liberation Army (SLA), etc.]

Historical background

Terrorism has its roots in first-century Palestine where Jewish Zealots publicly slit the throats of Romans and their collaborators. In seventh-century India, the Thuggee cult would ritually strangle passers-by as sacrifices to the Hindu deity Kali, and in the eleventh-century Middle East, a Shiite sect known as the Assassins were known to murder civilian foes while high on hashish. Scholars traced recognisably modern forms of terrorism back to such late-nineteenth-century organisations as Narodnaya Volya (People's Will), a Russian nihilist organisation, and its successor organisation, the Socialist Revolutionary Party.

There is no globally accepted definition of terrorism

Types of terrorism

Experts have identified at least four different types of terrorism:

A Nationalist-Separatist Terrorism: violence undertaken by those seeking to establish a separate state for their own national/ethnic group [e.g. the Irish Republican Army (IRA), Basque Homeland & Liberty (ETA), the Kurdish Workers Party (PKK)].

B Religious Terrorism: the use of violence by those seeking to further what they conceive as divinely commanded purposes, often targeting broad categories of 'enemies' in an attempt to bring about sweeping changes [e.g. Aum Shinrikyo, al-Qaida, Hizbollah, Hamas].

C Left-Wing Terrorism: violence undertaken by those seeking to destroy capitalism and replace it with a communist or socialist regime [e.g. Red Army Faction (RAF), German Red Brigades, Prima Linea, the Weather Underground/Symbionese Liberation Army].

D Right-Wing Terrorism: The use of violence by those seeking to dispense with liberal democratic governments [e.g. Timothy McVeigh].

⇨ Information from the US Foreign Policy Association. Visit www.fpa.org for more information.
© Foreign Policy Association

I wonder if that's Nationalist-Separatist, Religious, Left-Wing, or Right-Wing Terrorism?

Security and terrorism in the UK

Information from the Economic and Social Research Council

This information from the ESRC provides an overview of security apparatus and terrorism in the UK. Where appropriate, statistics are provided. However, due to the nature of the topic statistical information is limited. It is designed to be an introduction rather than a comprehensive overview. Other ESRC factsheets that are related to the issue of security and terrorism in the UK are *Global Security, Human rights, Crime in the UK.*

Terrorism

As a result of modern transportation, communication and access to resources, terrorism is becoming an ever-increasing threat. Terrorists are not recognised as belonging to any army and seek to weaken or supplant existing political landscapes for political, nationalist or religious goals using violence and intimidation.

Security

Security is the state of being or feeling secure. In this context, it refers to the state of, or safety of, the UK against criminal activity such as terrorism or espionage.

Counter-terrorism

The Home Office is the government department central to dealing with public safety including counter-terrorism. The Home Secretary is the head of the Home Office and is aided by six other government ministers.

The Foreign and Commonwealth Office works for UK interests overseas and is responsible for countering the international terrorist threat against UK.

Within this governmental structure there are a range of key departments and agencies whose job it is to keep the UK secure. These include: (1) the police, (2) military support to the police, (3) other law enforcement agencies, and (4) the security and intelligence services.

Intelligence and security services

The UK has three intelligence and security services:

⇨ The Secret Intelligence Service (SIS), also referred to as MI6, is responsible for secret intelligence and covert operations overseas.

⇨ The Security Service (MI5) is responsible for protecting the UK against threats to national security.

⇨ Government Communications Headquarters (GCHQ) works closely with SIS, MI5, the Ministry of Defence and law enforcement agencies to provide signal intelligence and keeps communication and information systems safe from hackers and other threats.

The Intelligence and Security Committee (ISC) examines the expenditure, administration and policy of the three agencies as a democratic safeguard to overseeing their work.

Government legislation that regulate the operations of the agencies

GCHQ and SIS adhere to the Intelligence Services Act 1994. The Security Service operates under the Security Services Acts 1989 and 1996. Their operations are also carried out in compliance with the Regulation of Investigatory Powers Act 2000.

Since the 9/11 attack on New York and the 7th July London bombings Parliament has passed a series of anti-terrorism bills including the Anti-Terrorism, Crime and Security Act 2001, the Prevention of Terrorism Act 2005 and the Terrorism Act 2006.

In 2004/05, international counter-terrorism accounted for 52 per cent of the security agencies' activities.

Spending since 2001

Since the terrorist attacks in America on 11th September 2001, funding for the security services has been significantly increased. An extra £775 million was made available in 2001 and by 2008 total spending is expected to have doubled to a figure of £2billion.

Figure 1 shows the capital and resource made available to security agencies through the Single Intelligence Account (SIA). Figures for 2006–2008 are planned expenditures.

Spending on services to cope with any emergency incidents has also been increased. There has been an increase of £85.5 million to the NHS to counter bio-terrorism; £56 million to the fire service decontamination programmes; £132 million to the fire service for search and rescue equipment; £49 million to the Metropolitan Police and £12 million to national police forces.

The work of the Security Service (MI5)

MI5 investigates threats to the UK by gathering, analysing and assessing intelligence. 87 per cent of MI5 resources work on counter-terrorism and protective security. Of this counter-terrorism activity, 60.5 per cent is international counter-terrorism and 16.5 per cent is domestic counter-terrorism. Other resources at MI5 are used for counter-espionage (6 per cent), counter-proliferation (2.5 per cent), external assistance (4 per cent – aiding SIS and GCHQ) and emerging and other threats (0.5 per cent).

The Security Service has no executive powers. Cases likely to result in prosecution are co-ordinated closely with the police, or Customs and Excise, who take the necessary action.

Proscribed groups

There are 44 proscribed international terrorist groups defined by the Terrorism Act 2000, which means they are outlawed in the UK. Of these two groups are proscribed under the Terrorism Act 2006, for glorifying terrorism. In addition, there are 14 organisations in Northern Ireland that are proscribed under the 2000 Act.

Changing nature of terrorism

Between 1990 and 2000 the number of people detained in connection with Irish terrorism under the prevention of terrorism legislation has declined significantly. At the last count in 2000, seven people were detained in connection with Irish terrorism, down from 12 in 1999, and the lowest number since 1974.

Since 2001, and especially after the London bombings of 7th July 2005, which killed 52 people and injured over 700 others, the perceived terrorist threat to the UK has changed significantly. This is tied to the rise of Al-Qaeda and its affiliated groups, which have resulted in a raft of new legislation and greatly increased activity by the security services. This work is centred on the enforcement of the Terrorism Act 2000, which was updated in 2006.

Terrorism Act 2000

The Terrorism Act 2000 replaced anti-terror legislations that dealt primarily with Northern Ireland. The New Act made many counter-terrorism measures which included:

Making terrorist groups illegal (proscription)

The Terrorism Act made it illegal for certain terrorist groups to operate in the UK and extended proscription to include international terrorist groups, like Al-Qaeda.

The Act enhanced police powers. Police were given greater powers to help prevent and investigate terrorism, including wider stop and search powers and the power to detain suspects after arrest for up to 28 days (periods of more than two days must be approved by a magistrate). This period was extended to 28 days under the Terrorism Act 2006

A number of new offences were introduced allowing police to arrest individuals suspected of inciting terrorist acts, seeking or providing training for terrorist purposes at home or overseas, providing instruction or training in the use of firearms, explosives or chemical, biological or nuclear weapons.

Police records indicate that between September 2001 and 30th September 2005, 895 people were arrested under the Terrorism Act 2000.

Figure 2 shows the outcomes of the 895 people arrested under the Terrorism Act 2000, between September 2001 and 30th September 2005.

Control orders

When suspected terrorists cannot be deported, the Prevention of Terrorism Act 2005 allows the Secretary of State to issue a 'control order' against an individual who 'he has reasonable grounds for suspecting is involved in terrorism-related activity and where he considers it necessary for the protection'. In July 2006, there were 15 control orders in operation. Nine of these were in respect of foreign nationals; the other six were in respect of British citizens.

Financial disruptions to terrorism

Since 2001, in relation to terrorist cases there have been:

⇨ £400,000 of cash seizures under the Anti-Terrorism, Crime and Security Act 2000;
⇨ £110,000 of forfeited funds;
⇨ £475,000 of funds seized under the Proceeds of Crime Act 2002; and
⇨ £477,000 subject to Treasury asset freezes.

(These figures do not include the £78 million that was frozen until 2002 as part of UK action against the Taliban.)
Updated 27 July 2007

⇨ The above information is reprinted with kind permission from the Economic and Social Research Council, the UK's leading research funding and training agency addressing economic and social concerns. Visit www.esrc.ac.uk for more information or to view references.
© ESRC

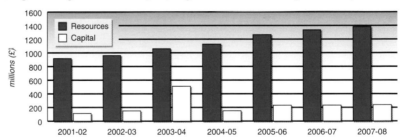

Security and terrorism in the UK

Figure 1: net annual resource and capital requirements for the agencies and Single Intelligence Account (SIA). Figures for 2006-08 are planned expenditures

Source: Intelligence and Security Committee Annual Report 2005-06 (2006) Cabinet Office, pp12 (Accessed 16 January 2007). Quoted in the ESRC factsheet 'Security and Terrorism in the UK'.

Figure 2: outcomes of the 895 people arrested under the Terrorism Act 2000, between September 2001 and 30th September 2005

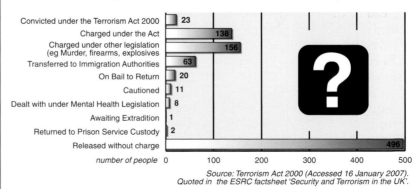

Source: Terrorism Act 2000 (Accessed 16 January 2007). Quoted in the ESRC factsheet 'Security and Terrorism in the UK'.

© Economic and Social Research Council

History of terrorism

From the first to the twenty-first century

What is terrorism?

Terrorism is distinguished from other acts of violence, and from war, by always having these four characteristics:

⇨ Terrorists violate the rules of modern warfare, established in acts called the Geneva Conventions and Hague Conventions; or they are actors (e.g., sub-state groups) who can't declare war legitimately;

⇨ Its goal is to achieve political change;

⇨ Its targets are symbolic of the political issue in question;

⇨ Acts of terror are designed to get attention from the public and media.

Terrorism in the pre-modern world

Violent acts on behalf of political change are as old as human history. The Sicarii were a first-century Jewish group who murdered enemies and collaborators in their campaign to oust their Roman rulers from Judea.

The Hashhashin, whose name gave us the English word 'assassins,' were a secretive Islamic sect active in Iran and Syria from the 11th to the 13th century.

By Amy Zalman, PhD

Their dramatically executed assassinations of Abbasid and Seljuk political figures terrified their contemporaries.

Zealots and assassins were not, however, really terrorists in the modern sense. Terrorism is best thought of as a modern phenomenon. Its characteristics flow from the international system of nation-states, and its success depends on the existence of a mass media to create an aura of terror among many people.

Violent acts on behalf of political change are as old as human history

1793: the origins of modern terrorism

The word terrorism comes from the Reign of Terror instigated by Maxmilien Robespierre in 1793, following the French revolution. Robespierre, one of twelve heads of the new state, had enemies of the revolution killed, and installed a dictatorship to stabilise the country. He justified his methods as necessary in the transformation of the monarchy to a liberal democracy:

'Subdue by terror the enemies of liberty, and you will be right, as founders of the Republic.'

Robespierre's sentiment laid the foundations for modern terrorists, who believe violence will usher in a better system. But the characterisation of terrorism as a state action faded, while the idea of terrorism as an attack against an existing political order became more prominent.

1950s: twentieth-century terror

The rise of guerrilla tactics by non-state actors in the last half of the twentieth century was due to several factors. These included the flowering of ethnic nationalism (e.g. Irish, Basque, Zionist), anti-colonial sentiments in the vast British, French and other empires, and new ideologies such as communism.

Terrorist groups with a nationalist agenda:

⇨ Irish Republican Army;

⇨ Kurdistan Workers' Party.

1970s: terrorism turns international

International terrorism is considered to have gotten its start at the 1972 Munich Olympics, at which a Palestinian organisation, Black September, kidnapped and killed Israeli athletes preparing to compete.

The event also gave us our contemporary sense of terrorism as highly theatrical, symbolic acts of violence by organised groups with specific political grievances.

Black September's political goal was negotiating the release of Palestinian prisoners. They used spectacular tactics to bring international attention to their national cause.

Munich radically changed the United States' handling of terrorism: 'The terms counter-

Post-7/7: preventing further attacks

Respondents were asked 'Which one or two, if any, of the following do you think would be most effective at preventing a possible terrorist attack on London's buses and tubes?'

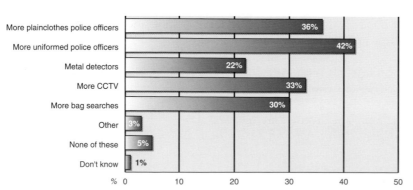

More plainclothes police officers	36%
More uniformed police officers	42%
Metal detectors	22%
More CCTV	33%
More bag searches	30%
Other	3%
None of these	5%
Don't know	1%

Based on 1,014 interviews conducted with a representative sample of Londoners aged 18+. Fieldwork 26th to 28th September 2005. Survey conducted by telephone using random dialling.

Source: Ipsos MORI, 5 October 2005

terrorism and international terrorism formally entered the Washington political lexicon,' according to counterterrorism expert Timothy Naftali.

Terrorists also took advantage of the black market in Soviet-produced light weaponry created in the wake of the Soviet Union's 1989 collapse. Most terrorist groups justified violence with a deep belief in the necessity and justice of their cause.

Terrorism in the United States also emerged. Groups such as the Weathermen grew out of the non-violent group Students for a Democratic Society. They turned to violent tactics, from rioting to setting off bombs, to protest against the Vietnam War.

International terrorism, notable attacks: 1968 PFLP hijacking of El Al Flight; 1988 Pan Am Lockerbie explosion.

1990s–21st century: religious terrorism and beyond

Religiously motivated terrorism is considered the most alarming terrorist threat today. Groups that justify their violence on Islamic grounds   Al Qaeda, Hamas, Hezbollah – come to mind first. But Christianity, Judaism, Hinduism and other religions have given rise to their own forms of militant extremism.

What is most distressing about this turn, as religion scholar Karen Armstrong points out, is terrorists' departure from any real religious precepts. Muhammad Atta, the architect of the 9/11 attacks, and 'the Egyptian hijacker who was driving the first plane, was a near alcoholic and was drinking vodka before he boarded the aircraft'. Alcohol would be strictly off limits for a highly observant Muslim.

Atta, and perhaps many others, are not simply orthodox believers turned violent, but rather violent extremists who manipulate religious concepts for their own purposes.

Timeline: terrorism threats to the UK

UK terror attacks, threats and scares since 2001. By Tom Gregory

December 2001: The shoebomber
Briton Richard Reid attempts to bring down a jetliner over the Atlantic with explosives concealed in his shoe. He is restrained by passengers and later sentenced to life imprisonment in the US.

August 2002: Armed man on Ryanair flight
Swedish police arrest a man at Vasteraas airport near Stockholm as he tries to board a London-bound Ryanair flight carrying a gun. The suspect, Kerim Chatty, had also enrolled for flying lessons in the US. Hijacking charges against Chatty were dropped but the Swedish courts imprisoned him for weapons offences.

January 2003: Ricin plot
Police in north London discover the raw ingredients required for the production of ricin but none of the actual toxin is found. Nine people are arrested. Kamel Bourgass is jailed for plotting to spread poisons and for murdering Detective Constable Stephen Oake. The prosecution provides no evidence against four men and they are acquitted. The other four men are found not guilty of involvement in the plot.

February 2003: Tanks at Heathrow
About 450 troops and over 1,000 police are deployed at Heathrow airport after intelligence reports suggest that terrorists are planning a missile attack on a passenger jet.

September 2004: Red mercury
Police arrest four men after a tip-off from *News of the World* reporter Mazher Mahmood about an alleged plot to purchase and use red mercury in a 'dirty bomb' attack. The men are later acquitted at trial.

November 2004: Canary Wharf plot
The *Daily Mail* and ITV claim that security services have uncovered a plot to fly a plane into Canary Wharf. Senior Whitehall officials initially deny the claims but a recent US report alleges that the building was an al-Qaida target.

7 July 2005: London suicide attacks
Four British suicide bombers kill 52 passengers on the London public transport network.

21 July 2005: Failed bomb attempts in London
Seven men are expected to go on trial in September in relation to their alleged involvement in a plot to bomb three tube trains and a bus.

22 July 2005: Stockwell shooting
Brazilian Jean Charles de Menezes is shot and killed by police who mistakenly believe he is a suicide bomber.

June 2006: Forest Gate terror raid
Over 250 police storm a house in Forest Gate, east London, and arrest two brothers on suspicion of involvement in a planned biological attack. One of the arrested, Mohammed Abdul Kahar, is shot in the shoulder during the raid. The brothers are released without charge.

August 2006: Aircraft terror plot uncovered
The home secretary, John Reid, says a plot was disrupted to cause civilian casualties on an 'unprecedented scale' by detonating explosives on up to 10 transatlantic flights from UK airports.
10 August 2006

Attitudes to terrorist attacks post-London bombings

Results of an Ipsos MORI survey carried out after the London tube bombings in July 2005

How likely do you think it is that London will experience another terrorist attack in the near future? Would you say it is . . .

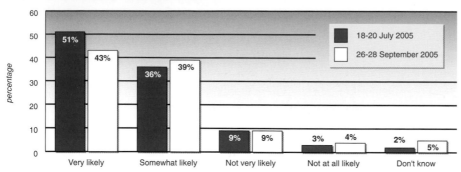

	Very likely	Somewhat likely	Not very likely	Not at all likely	Don't know
18-20 July 2005	51%	36%	9%	3%	2%
26-28 September 2005	43%	39%	9%	4%	5%

As a result of the attacks in London in July this year have you spent more time or less time in Central London, or have the attacks made no difference at all?

	Some time	At least once a month	At least once a week
More time	2%	2%	2%
Less time	21%	20%	17%
Made no difference	77%	77%	80%
Don't know	*	*	*

Have you stopped completely bringing your children into Central London for fear of terrorist attacks?

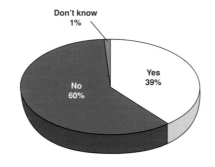

Don't know 1%
Yes 39%
No 60%

As a result of the attacks, have you considered moving to live outside of London or not?

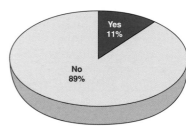

Yes 11%
No 89%

Source: Ipsos MORI, 5 October 2005.

Facts and figures

Information from the Home Office

The UK police terrorism arrest statistics (excluding Northern Ireland) from 11 September 2001 to 31 March 2007 show 1228 arrests were made:
⇨ 1165 arrests under the Terrorism Act 2000;
⇨ 63 arrests under legislation other than the Terrorism Act, where the investigation was conducted as a terrorist investigation.
   Of the total 1228 arrested:
⇨ 132 charged with terrorism legislation offences only;
⇨ 109 charged with terrorism legislation offences and other criminal offences;
⇨ 195 charged under other legislation including murder, grievous bodily harm, firearms, explosives offences, fraud, false documents;
⇨ 76 handed over to immigration authorities;
⇨ 15 on police bail awaiting charging decisions;
⇨ 1 warrant issued for arrest;
⇨ 12 cautioned;
⇨ 1 dealt with under youth offending procedures
⇨ 11 dealt with under mental health legislation
⇨ 4 transferred to Police Service of Northern Ireland

custody;
⇨ 2 remanded in custody awaiting extradition proceedings;
⇨ 669 released without charge;
⇨ 1 awaiting further investigation.
   Of those charged:
⇨ 41 Terrorism Act convictions to date;
⇨ 183 convicted under other legislation: murder and explosives offences (including conspiracies), grievous bodily harm, firearms offences, fraud, false documents offences, etc. (this includes the 12 cautions detailed above);
⇨ 114 at or awaiting trial.
(Source: These statistics are compiled from police records by the offices of the National Coordinator for Terrorist Investigations. They are subject to change as cases go through the system.)

⇨ The above information is reprinted with kind permission from the Home Office. Visit www.homeoffice.gov.uk for more information.

© Crown copyright

Head of MI5: terror threat is growing

Information from the Home Office

In a speech to the Society of Editors, the Director General of the Security Service, Jonathan Evans, outlined the threats the UK faces.

The nation's main security threat remains al Qaida and groups related to it, Mr Evans said.

And the root of that threat is an extremist ideology 'whose basic tenets are inimical to the tolerance and liberty that form the basis of our democracy,' he said.

The threat continues to grow

He said the number of known extremists within the UK who security services believe could pose a threat was increasing steadily.

'In her speech this time last year, my predecessor, Eliza Manningham-Buller, pointed out that this country was facing an increasing threat from al Qaida-inspired terrorism. When she spoke, MI5 had identified around 1,600 individuals who we believed posed a direct threat to national security and public safety, because of their support for terrorism.

'That figure today would be at least 2,000,' he said.

That increase could be attributed in part to good work on the part of security services, but there is also 'a steady flow of new recruits to the extremist cause'.

Some of those recruits are very young.

Children, he said, should be protected from extremism in the same way they are protected from other types of exploitation.

'As I speak, terrorists are methodically and intentionally targeting young people and children in this country,' Mr Evans said. 'They are radicalising, indoctrinating and grooming young, vulnerable people to carry out acts of terrorism. This year, we have seen individuals as young as 15 and 16 implicated in terrorist-related activity.'

A deliberate, dynamic campaign

Al Qaida is conducting a deliberate campaign against the UK, he said. Its hostility towards the UK existed long before 11 September 2001. That same hostility is clear in the papers left behind by actual and would-be bombers. And it regularly forms part of al Qaida's broadcast messages.

The terrorism campaign is dynamic, and over the last year it has evolved.

'It is important that we recognise an uncomfortable truth: terrorist attacks we have seen against the UK are not simply random plots by disparate and fragmented groups. The majority of these attacks, successful or otherwise, have taken place because al Qaida has a clear determination to mount terrorist attacks against the United Kingdom. This remains the case today, and there is no sign of it reducing.'

Given al Qaida's recent expansion from Pakistan into Somalia and Algeria, he said, he does not believe the threat to the UK has 'yet reached its peak'.

Rejecting extremism is the key

The security services, he said, will do their best to prevent attacks in the UK, but alone, that is merely containment.

Long-term resolution of the problem will require identifying and addressing the root causes of the threat. 'This is not a job only for the intelligence agencies and police. It requires a collective effort in which Government, faith communities and wider civil society have an important part to play.'

Success would begin when people reject violent extremist ideology. And that, he said, will not happen overnight.

The problem with that, though, is ensuring that the press, the public and the government understand the nature of the battle they face.

'We know that the strategic thinking of our enemies is long-term. But public discourse in the UK works to a much shorter timescale – whether the electoral cycle or the media deadline. We cannot view this challenge in such timescales. If we only react tactically while our enemies plan strategically, we shall be hard put to win this.

'A key part of our strategy must be perseverance.'

You can read Mr Evan's speech in full on MI5's website.
5 November 2007

⇨ Information from the Home Office. Visit www.homeoffice.gov.uk for more information.
© *Crown copyright*

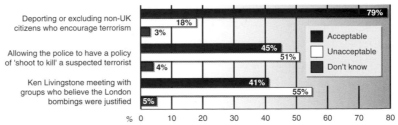

Measures against terrorists

Respondents were asked 'On balance, for each of the following statements I read out, please tell me whether you think they are acceptable or unacceptable?'

Deporting or excluding non-UK citizens who encourage terrorism: 79%, 18%, 3%

Allowing the police to have a policy of 'shoot to kill' a suspected terrorist: 45%, 51%, 4%

Ken Livingstone meeting with groups who believe the London bombings were justified: 41%, 55%, 5%

■ Acceptable □ Unacceptable ■ Don't know

% 0 10 20 30 40 50 60 70 80

Based on 1,014 interviews conducted with a representative sample of Londoners aged 18+. Fieldwork 26th to 28th September 2005. Survey conducted by telephone using random dialling. Source: Ipsos MORI, 5 October 2005

Terrorists and the Internet

Information from the US Council on Foreign Relations

By Eben Kaplan,
Associate Editor

Introduction

Terrorists increasingly are using the Internet as a means of communication both with each other and the rest of the world. By now, nearly everyone has seen at least some images from propaganda videos published on terrorist sites and rebroadcast on the world's news networks. Western governments have intensified surveillance of such sites but their prosecution of site operators is hampered by concerns over civil liberties, the Internet's inherent anonymity, and other factors.

How do terrorist organisations use the Internet?

The Internet is a powerful tool for terrorists, who use online message boards and chat rooms to share information, coordinate attacks, spread propaganda, raise funds, and recruit, experts say. According to Haifa University's Gabriel Weimann, whose research on the subject is widely cited, over the last ten years the number of terrorist sites has jumped from less than 100 to more than 4,800. 'This has particularly taken off since the war in Iraq, as many of the insurgency groups there have many sites and message boards to help their network,' says Michael Kern, a senior analyst at the SITE Institute, a Washington-based terrorist-tracking group.

Terrorist websites can serve as virtual training grounds, offering tutorials on building bombs, firing surface-to-air missiles, shooting at US soldiers, and sneaking into Iraq from abroad. Terrorist sites also host messages and propaganda videos which help to raise morale and further the expansion of recruitment and fundraising networks.

What constitutes a 'terrorist website'?

Defining a terrorist website is as contentious as defining terrorism. A team of Pentagon analysts recently testified before Congress that they monitor some 5,000 jihadi websites, though they closely watch a small number of these – less than 100 – that are deemed the most hostile.

Terrorist sites include the official sites of designated terrorist organisations, as well as the sites of supporters, sympathisers, and fans, says Weimann. But when websites with no formal terrorist affiliation contain sympathetic sentiments to the political aims of a terrorist group, the definition becomes murky. Hoax sites can also prove a troublesome red herring for monitors of terrorist sites.

How effective is online terrorist propaganda?

Perhaps the most effective way in which terrorists use the Internet is the spread of propaganda. Abu Musab al-Zarqawi's al-Qaeda cell in Iraq has proven particularly adept in its use of the web, garnering attention by posting footage of events such as roadside bombings, the decapitation of American hostage Nick Berg, and kidnapped Egyptian and Algerian diplomats prior to their execution. On 29 July, the Iraqi al-Qaeda group released via the Internet a forty-six-minute propaganda video entitled 'All Religion Will Be for Allah'. The *Washington Post* report described it as 'slickly produced' with 'the feel of a blood-and-guts annual report'.

In Iraq, experts say terrorist propaganda videos are viewed by a large portion of society, not just those who sympathise with terrorists and insurgents. In addition to being posted online, the videos are said to be sold in Baghdad video shops, hidden behind the counter along with pornography. Evan Kohlmann, an expert in terrorists' use of the Internet, points out that propaganda films are not exclusively made in the Middle East; groups from Bosnia, Afghanistan, and Chechnya have also produced videos. Nor are videos the only form of propaganda. As Pentagon analysts told a 4 May hearing of the US House Intelligence Committee, some jihadi websites offer video games in which users as young as seven can pretend to be holy warriors killing US soldiers.

In 2004, General John Abizaid, the head of US Central Command, told reporters terrorist websites cleverly 'develop the perception of great strength' and project a 'virtual caliphate' [theocracy based on Islamic law] to thousands of viewers around the globe.

What advantages does the Internet offer terrorists?

'The greatest advantage [of the Internet] is stealth,' says John Arquilla, professor of defence analysis at the Naval Postgraduate School. '[Terrorists] swim in an ocean of bits and bytes.' Terrorists have developed sophisticated encryption tools and creative techniques that make the Internet an efficient and relatively secure means of correspondence. These include steganography, a technique used to hide messages in graphic files, and 'dead dropping': transmitting information through saved email drafts in an online email account accessible to anyone with the password.

The Internet also provides a global pool of potential recruits and donors. Online terrorist fundraising has become so commonplace that some organisations are able to accept donations via the popular online payment service, PayPal.

What is cyberterrorism?

Cyberterrorism is typically defined as the use of the Internet as a vehicle through which to launch an attack. Terrorists could conceivably hack into electrical grids and security systems, or perhaps distribute a powerful computer virus. 'Al-Qaeda operatives are known to have taken training in hacking techniques,' Arquilla says, but the likelihood of such a cyber attack seems fairly remote. While hackers have created their fair share of online mischief, not one instance in the United States has been confirmed as an act of cyberterrorism.

Kohlmann suggests the established definition of cyberterrorism needs to be broadened. He says any application of terrorism on the Internet should be considered cyberterrorism. 'There's no distinction between the online [terrorist] community and the real [terrorist] community.' As evidence, Kohlmann recounts one extreme instance in which the Iraqi insurgent group Army of the Victorious Sect held a contest to help design the group's new website. According to Kohlmann, the prize for the winning designer was the opportunity to, with the click of a mouse, remotely fire three rockets at a US military base in Iraq.

Who are the most prominent online terrorists?

The most infamous figure in the world of online terrorism is 'Irhaby 007' ('Terrorist 007'). As a SITE Institute profile explains, Irhaby 007 was celebrated by other online terrorists for his hacking prowess and his ability to securely distribute information. With his assistance, terrorist organisations around the globe were able to expand the reach of their message. Irhaby 007 passed this knowledge along to other online jihadis through web postings such as his 'Seminar for Hacking Websites', creating a network of technology-savvy terrorist disciples. In October 2005, Scotland Yard officers in West London arrested 22-year-old Younis Tsouli, whom they later identified as Irhaby 007. Tsouli is awaiting trial on charges that include conspiracy to murder and terrorist fundraising.

Another prominent online terrorist is Abu Maysarah al-Iraqi, who serves as the media representative for al-Qaeda in Iraq leader Zarqawi. Al-Iraqi goes online to claim responsibility for acts of terrorism, post propaganda videos, and issue statements on behalf of Zarqawi, though experts say it is unclear whether al-Iraqi is just one person or several using the same name. Kohlmann says the number of prominent online terrorists is dwindling; they are being replaced by 'an army of smaller guys who are completely replaceable'.

The 'Baghdad Sniper' or 'Juba' is a different kind of online terrorist. Juba is a well-trained, efficient sniper who stalks and kills US soldiers in Baghdad and then posts videos of the killings on the web. 'Everyone has got him in the back of their minds,' US Specialist Travis Burress told the *Guardian*. 'He's a serious threat to us.' According to one such video, Juba and his fellow snipers killed 143 US soldiers and injured fifty-four over a one-year period starting in autumn 2004.

How do governments respond to terrorists' online activities?

There is some debate within the counterterrorism community about how to combat terrorist sites. 'The knee-jerk reaction is if you see a terrorist site you shut it down,' Kohlmann says, but doing so can cause investigators to miss out on a wealth of valuable information. 'You can see who's posting what and who's paying for it,' Kern says. For instance, German officials monitoring online chatter issued early warnings prior to the Madrid train bombings in March 2004.

Shutting down a terrorist website is just a temporary disruption. To truly stop a terrorist site, experts say, the webmaster must be stopped. The ability of the US National Security Agency to monitor such individuals inside the United States has been the subject of a heated political and legal debate. The United States has tried to prosecute webmasters who run terrorist websites in the West, but has run into opposition from advocates of free speech. 'Sites that tell the terrorist side of the story go right up to the brink of civil liberties,' Arquilla says. Sami Omar al-Hussayen, a Saudi Arabian graduate student at the University of Idaho, was charged by US officials with supporting terrorism because he served as a webmaster for several Islamic groups whose sites linked to organisations praising terrorist attacks in Chechnya and Israel. Al-Hussayen was acquitted of all terrorism charges by a federal court in June 2004 under the First Amendment. Two months later, Babar Ahmad, a 31-year-old, British-born son of Pakistani immigrants, was arrested in London under a US warrant. Ahmad, whose case is ongoing, is charged with running a network of websites spreading propaganda and fundraising for the Taliban, Chechen rebels, and al-Qaeda affiliates. His supporters claim extradition would violate his rights as a British citizen.

Another approach officials have taken is to create phony terrorist websites. These can spread disinformation, such as instructions for building a bomb that will explode prematurely and kill its maker or false intelligence about the location of US forces in Iraq, intended to lead terrorist fighters into a trap. This tactic must be used sparingly, says Kohlmann, or else officials risk 'poisoning a golden pot [of information]' about how terrorists operate.
Updated 12 May 2006

⇨ From CFR.org, a US-based nonpartisan resource for information and analysis. Reprinted with permission. For more analysis and backgrounders on terrorism and US foreign policy, go to www.cfr.org

We are offering the terrorist a megaphone

Hysteria politics feasts on the threat of violence, and accords the status of political crusader to the common criminal

Don't panic. Stay calm. Don't play the terrorist's game. Show no fear or sense of disruption. Don't change your behaviour or way of life. Pass no laws curbing freedom. Just shrug and go about your normal business.

Omigod! Now they are doctors! Wake the prime minister, round up the Arabs and order armoured helicopters. Stop the presses and clear the schedules. The fiends from outer Asia are cunning. They could be poisoning hospital drips. They could be lacing paracetamol and putting anthrax in Elastoplast. Declare another bomb 'imminent'. Surround Heathrow with tanks, fortify Wimbledon, put blast blocks round Waterloo and ack-ack guns on Parliament Hill. Raise the threat level from critical to panic. On second thoughts make that totally hysterical.

'Doctor Evil', cries the *Sun*, demanding we 'Rip up the hated human rights act'. 'Docs of War', chimes the *Mirror*, discarding 'innocent until proved guilty'. 'Terror cell in the NHS', shrieks the *Express*. Nor is the rest of the media much better. Fed by anonymous security officials eager to boast of their successes, almost all reports have contrived to link the bombs with al-Qaida, 9/11, the NHS, mayhem and martyrdom.

The public realm in Britain is in rampant retreat before terrorism, largely because politicians and the media feast on any story involving actual or potential violence. Politicians want to present themselves as calm and statesmanlike, yet visible, defenders of public security, as their poll ratings soar. Gordon Brown's 'strength' rating jumped 14 points in a *Times*/Populus poll yesterday. The media can revel in fear journalism, throwing all sense of

By Simon Jenkins

proportion to the winds and filling pages and airwaves with speculation as to what 'might have happened if ...' and what 'could yet happen unless ...', scanning that horizon so appetising to every news desk: the worst-case scenario. The BBC re-enacts a Pythonesque sketch with a white-haired boffin igniting a can of petrol in a sandpit and remarking that it could have been a thousand times worse. The word suspect has become synonymous with mass murderer.

> **The public realm in Britain is in rampant retreat before terrorism, largely because politicians and the media feast on any story involving actual or potential violence**

The sanest person last Friday was the reviled Downing Street official who decided not to wake the prime minister at two in the morning to tell him of suspect cars in the West End. Nobody was dead. The police were on the case. The home secretary had been woken (a deed apparently vital to any anti-terror operation). Matters would be clearer by breakfast. Leave the poor man his sleep.

Gordon Brown was reportedly furious at not being disturbed. Hysteria politics demands that the prime minister be roused in the middle

of the night. Under the old regime, Tony Blair and John Reid would have been jostling in front of the cameras, promising 10 new crackdowns by lunchtime. Yet here was Brown in the land of nod while his new home secretary, Jacqui Smith, was winning headlines for looking concerned and cool.

To be fair, Brown's new team did not imitate Blair with a battery of instant illiberal initiatives. Three amateurish car bombs were dealt with by the public, police and security services, each playing its role with efficiency and bravery. As in the case of the IRA bombing campaign, my impression is that a richly resourced security apparatus is getting on top of the current bombing menace. It and the public can cope.

British national security is not remotely threatened by these bombs. They do not, as Blair loved to claim, 'undermine the British way of life and threaten western civilisation'. They

kill people and damage property. When last November Mr Justice Butterfield sentenced the terrorist Dhiren Barot to life imprisonment for conspiracy to murder, he felt obliged ludicrously to elevate a criminal into an Islamist hero and martyr by accusing him of 'seeking the means to bring death and destruction to the western world ... striking at the heart of democracy ... and ultimately the whole nation of the US and the UK'.

Such Nuremberg histrionics are exactly what Islamist terrorism craves. The worst the present crop of maniacs appears able to do is kill people. This is deplorable, but death happens daily to innocent people on Britain's streets, from which police are being withdrawn under Home Office pressure 'to counter terrorism'. While the concept of the suicide bomber has given a new menace to the history of political violence, the change is quantitative rather than qualitative.

There is no doubt of the murderous intent of the cells operating in Britain. But they have no sensible answer in the villages of Pakistan, the streets of Basra or the Strait of Hormuz. There is no answer in the Ministry of Defence or in that liberal cliché,

the hearts and minds of Britain's Muslim population, which are as overwhelmingly opposed to them as the rest of Britain. The answer lies only in normal crime-busting, in patient and intelligent policing, and in accepting that every now and then a bomber will get through. Very few do and adequate steps are being taken to minimise the risk without the need for some new Draco at the Home Office.

Death happens daily to innocent people on Britain's streets, from which police are being withdrawn . . . 'to counter terrorism'

Where there is no cause for confidence is in the response of politicians and public comment. Terrorism cannot work without the fear engendered by publicity and the clamour for revenge. The terrorist wants a megaphone for his cause, 'understanding' for his grievance,

and martyrdom for himself and his colleagues. He wants what the IRA demanded and British governments initially refused (before capitulating): the status of political crusader rather than common criminal. Today every statement from government, judiciary and press accords terrorists that status.

Nobody seems to know what, where or who al-Qaida is, yet the name is used to dust with global significance any bomb plot anywhere. Brown spoke of the car bombs as 'al-Qaida-linked in motivation and ideology'. Why so glorify them? It is like linking a bank raid in the Old Kent Road 'to the global mafia in motivation and ideology'. Why err on the side of terror rather than on the side of calm? Fear pumped up to the level of panic by the oxygen of publicity is precisely what the terrorist wants.

If Brown wants to turn over a new leaf in the campaign to contain the Islamist menace he should leave it to the police. He should have set the nation an example and been happy to remain asleep.

4 July 2007
© *Guardian Newspapers Limited 2007*

Living apart together

Statistics taken from the Policy Exchange report *Living apart together – British Muslims and the paradox of multiculturalism*

'I feel more in common with Muslims in other countries than I do with non-Muslims in Britain'

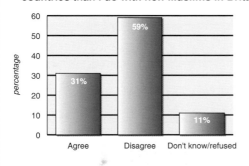

'I admire organisations like Al-Qaeda that are prepared to fight against the West' – by age group

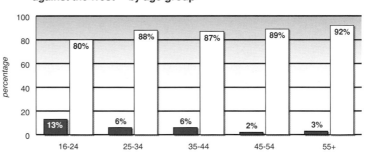

'Many of the problems in the world today are a result of arrogant western attitudes' (Muslim population)

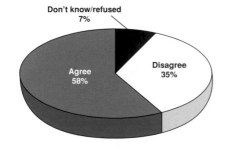

'Many of the problems in the world today are a result of arrogant western attitudes' (General population)

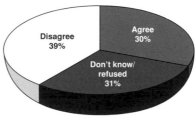

Source: Policy Exchange, January 2007.

Fear of terrorism

At least one in seven UK adults is fearful of having children because of the looming threat of terrorism, a new survey has revealed

The YouGov study, carried out for the Mental Health Foundation in conjunction with World Mental Health Day (Wednesday, 10th October), showed that global troubles were worrying enough to inspire 15 per cent of adults to put off starting a family.

Some 70 per cent of the 2,012 respondents admitted that terrorism was their biggest worry, while 58 per cent of those surveyed admitted to being regularly concerned by immigration.

But while one in four participants found having an electoral voice a big help in coping with their anxieties, 30 per cent were resigned to continually being worried.

Clinical psychologist Dr Michael Reddy explained why terrorism was revealed to be more of a worry than environmental concerns such as climate change.

'As social animals, we are sensitive to dangers from other humans that are intentional, such as terrorism,' he said.

'Accidental dangers, such as natural disasters, fail to motivate us in the same way.'

He added: 'Feeling a threat to one's group from an unknown force, such as immigration, can threaten this sense of security and make people feel anxious.'

Dr Andrew McCulloch, chief executive of the Mental Health Foundation, commented: 'If angst is reaching a level where adults are contemplating whether or not to have children, then this could be a serious mental health issue because the current global issues aren't going away in a hurry.

'To help lessen any worry, a person should find out more about the issue that is concerning them and talk to others about it.'

The online survey, carried out between 1st and 3rd August, found that world events left UK adults feeling powerless (56%), angry (50%), anxious (35%) and depressed (26%). 8 October 2007

© Adfero Ltd

How worried are people about terrorism?

Key statistics from the Global Issues Survey, undertaken in August 2007. The world is currently facing a number of different threats that leave some people feeling frustrated, powerless and anxious. Even if a threat poses very little actual risk, the worry is still real and can impact on a person's day-to-day life and mental wellbeing. We have done some research looking into how global issues are affecting the mental health and behaviour of some people.

When people were asked which global issues worry them most:

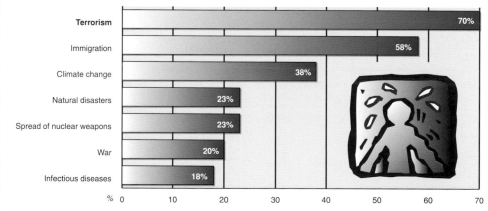

Issue	%
Terrorism	70%
Immigration	58%
Climate change	38%
Natural disasters	23%
Spread of nuclear weapons	23%
War	20%
Infectious diseases	18%

When people were asked what helps them to deal with their worry about global issues:

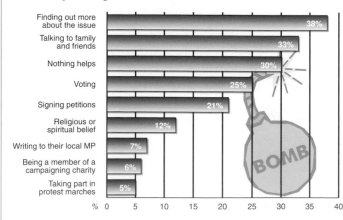

Help	%
Finding out more about the issue	38%
Talking to family and friends	33%
Nothing helps	30%
Voting	25%
Signing petitions	21%
Religious or spiritual belief	12%
Writing to their local MP	7%
Being a member of a campaigning charity	6%
Taking part in protest marches	5%

When asked what emotions people feel as a result of global issues:

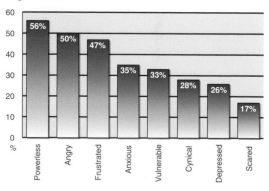

Emotion	%
Powerless	56%
Angry	50%
Frustrated	47%
Anxious	35%
Vulnerable	33%
Cynical	28%
Depressed	26%
Scared	17%

Base: 2012. Reproduced from the Mental Health Foundation website with their permission. Find out more at http://www.mentalhealth.org.uk/campaigns

New UK terror threat from foreign students

By Brendan Carlin, John Steele and Duncan Gardham

The new crackdown on terrorism following the attempted car bomb attacks is 'fatally flawed' amid fears of widespread failings on immigration checks, the Government was warned last night.

As new concerns were raised that the intelligence services are struggling to monitor more than 200 extremist groups operating in Britain, it emerged that a loophole on student visas could allow terrorists in.

Many students from 'hot spots' of Muslim unrest around the world are thought to obtain visas for study but 'go under the wire' by failing to show up for their courses when they arrive in Britain.

The head of Interpol also accused the authorities of failing to check visitors to Britain against its global database of 11,000 suspected terrorists.

Amid warnings that the terrorist threat could last a generation, Gordon Brown sought to adopt a strong position on combating the threat by calling yesterday for a new world-wide database on suspects.

The Prime Minister has been warned that the terrorist threat could 'last a generation'

Data-sharing between countries was 'a matter of urgency', the Prime Minister said.

But the Tories warned that any crackdown was in danger of being undermined by a failure to monitor immigrants.

They said that without tackling immigration issues such as this, Mr Brown's overall strategy against terrorism was 'fatally flawed'.

A Tory spokesman said the student visa loophole had to be closed as soon as possible.

Damian Green, a shadow Home Office minister, told the *Daily Telegraph*: 'If someone does not show up for their course and explain immediately, their visas should be cancelled at once. It's an appalling loophole that the Government has to deal with urgently.'

Many students from 'hot spots' of Muslim unrest around the world are thought to obtain visas for study but 'go under the wire' by failing to show up for their courses

David Davis, the shadow home secretary, said: 'We welcome the Prime Minister's sentiments but they are undermined by the revelation that Britain is not checking potential immigrants against an existing global database of terror suspects.

'Yet again it is not the Government's policy that is the problem – it is their lack of competence in delivering on that policy which is threatening our security.'

Mr Davis was referring to a claim by Ronald K. Noble, the Interpol secretary general, who said it had the passport numbers, fingerprints and photos of more than 11,000 suspected terrorists on its database.

But he said Britain does not check it against immigrants coming into the country or foreign nationals it has arrested.

'The guys detained last week could be wanted, arrested or convicted anywhere in the world and the UK would not know,' he said.

Mr Brown's call came as his new security minister, Adml Sir Alan West, told the *Sunday Telegraph* that the fight against terrorism could take 15 years.

Following the car bomb attacks in London and Glasgow, Sir Alan said the overall threat, from both home-grown and foreign terrorists, was now at its greatest-ever level.

Yesterday it emerged that MI5 is attempting to monitor more than 200 extremist networks across the country. The security service is watching 219 groups, mostly in the Midlands and North.

Relations between Muslims and non-Muslims

Participants were asked to respond to the statement 'I feel that I have as much in common with non-Muslims as I do with Muslims'.

Don't know/refused
5%

Disagree
29%

Agree
66%

Source: statistic taken from the Policy Exchange report Living apart together – British Muslims and the paradox of multiculturalism.
© Policy Exchange 2007

A 'risk map' of terrorist threats shows a total of 80 groups of extremists in the Midlands, 60 in Leeds, Bradford and Manchester and 35 in London.

There are also 20 being watched on Merseyside, 12 in Scotland, 10 in Wales and two in Northern Ireland.

Each network can involve more than a dozen people bringing the total to well over 1,600 – some estimates have put it as high as 3,000.

Most are not involved in plotting attacks but the security service is alarmed at the increasing speed with which groups move from radicalisation to action.

It is struggling to monitor all the networks and is unable to keep all the people under constant surveillance. Some are believed to move away from their homes to more remote locations as they finalise their plans, to avoid being watched.

Dame Eliza Manningham-Buller, while still head of MI5, said last year that there had been an 80 per cent rise in its casework.

She said MI5 was monitoring around 200 groupings or networks comprising more than 1,600 individuals 'who are actively engaged in plotting or facilitating terrorist acts here and overseas'.

To help fight the threat outside London, regional counter-terrorism units have been set up in Birmingham, Manchester and Leeds to work with the Metropolitan Police in London.

Sir Alan, the former First Sea Lord brought in from outside the Labour Party by Mr Brown to serve in his 'all the talents' administration, said people would now have to be 'a little un-British' and if necessary, inform on each other to trap suspected terrorists.

He will today present Mr Brown and Jacqui Smith, the Home Secretary, with a hastily-prepared interim report on vetting arrangements for NHS staff after it emerged that eight of the suspects in the London and Glasgow attacks worked for the health service.

One report said that in Portsmouth University alone, hundreds of foreign students who were offered places failed to turn up

---

The report was only commissioned last Wednesday although Mr Brown has already told MPs that background checks on foreign doctors and other health workers coming to Britain will be stepped up.

However, deep concerns were raised over the weekend that a loophole in visa controls for foreign students could have been letting in extremists without real checks.

One report yesterday said that in Portsmouth University alone, hundreds of foreign students who were offered places failed to turn up.

Of those, 379 were from Pakistan, 16 from Saudi Arabia and two from Iraq.

Until recently, a student could obtain a visa for up to three years essentially by showing an acceptance letter.

The Home Office said last night it had taken steps to close what it accepted was a 'loophole' open to abuse.

Foreign students would now have to show details of a 'sponsor' who will certify that they have been offered a place. The sponsors will have to report any who fail to show up.

10 July 2007
© *Telegraph Group Limited, London 2007*

Islam, terrorism and September 11

Information from the Forum Against Islamophobia and Racism (FAIR)

Islam is frequently misunderstood in some parts of the world today. Perhaps this is because religion no longer dominates everyday life in Western society; whereas, for Muslims, Islam is life. Muslims make no distinction between the secular and the sacred.

The impact of various global events involving Muslims has also meant that Islam and Muslims are more frequently covered in media news reporting. The result is that Muslims everywhere are seen through the same negative stereotypes that have somewhat clouded the reality of the situation, where Islamic terms such as 'jihad', 'fatwa' and 'fundamentalist' are now part of popular vocabulary, albeit with a new 'media-ised' meaning.

Jihad is inaccurately used only to mean a 'holy war'

Part of this has seen the worrying development of linking of Islam and Muslims with terrorism. Whilst September 11th proliferated this through inappropriate media coverage attributing the attacks indiscriminately against Muslims, it was noticeable prior to this one date where the uses of 'Islamic terrorist', 'militant Islam' and 'Muslim extremist' were all quite common. In some respects, the term 'Islamic fundamentalist' had become popularly but quite incorrectly interchangeable with 'Islamic terrorist'.

With regards to terrorism, Islam respects the sacredness of life, and rejects any express statement or tacit insinuation that Muslims should harm innocent people: 'If one takes a life, it is as if one has taken the life of all humanity. If one saves a single

F·A·I·R

FORUM AGAINST ISLAMOPHOBIA & RACISM

life, it is as if he has saved the life of all humanity' (inspired by Qur'an 5:32).

FAIR therefore, as do the vast majority of peace-loving Muslims here in the UK and elsewhere, wholeheartedly condemns all terrorism and has sought to make this very clear message at every opportunity. FAIR also believes however that the actions of an individual or a small group do not necessarily represent the beliefs of a particular religion nor its many adherents, and the religion itself cannot be held responsible for such actions. In reality, Islam not only condemns terrorism and suicide missions, but also prohibits them completely.

Fatwa
The opinion, under Islamic law of a pious or knowledgeable Islamic scholar. The fatwa is only relevant to those who follow or are taught by that particular scholar – it is NOT for ALL Muslims.

Fundamentalist
A term originally coined to describe certain Christians in America. The inappropriateness of its popular usage is highlighted by the fact that most Muslims would describe themselves as fundamentalist, due to their belief in the fundamentals of Islam. It is NOT the case that ALL Muslims are engaged in conflict or war.

Jihad
Meaning self-purification and derives from the term for the need to strive, struggle, exert oneself and to be willing to overcome evil for good. This is commonly misinterpreted where jihad is inaccurately used only to mean a 'holy war'.

↪ The above information is reprinted with kind permission from the Forum Against Islamophobia and Racism. Visit www.fairuk.org for more information.

© FAIR

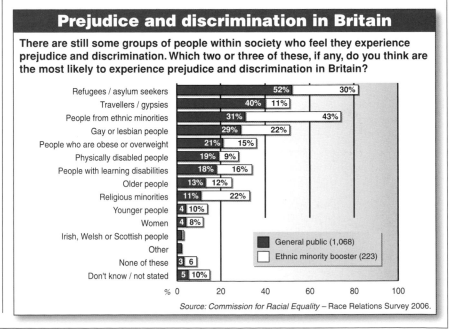

Prejudice and discrimination in Britain

There are still some groups of people within society who feel they experience prejudice and discrimination. Which two or three of these, if any, do you think are the most likely to experience prejudice and discrimination in Britain?

	General public (1,068)	Ethnic minority booster (223)
Refugees / asylum seekers	52%	30%
Travellers / gypsies	40%	11%
People from ethnic minorities	31%	43%
Gay or lesbian people	29%	22%
People who are obese or overweight	21%	15%
Physically disabled people	19%	9%
People with learning disabilities	18%	16%
Older people	13%	12%
Religious minorities	11%	22%
Younger people	4	10%
Women	4	8%
Irish, Welsh or Scottish people		
Other		
None of these	3	6
Don't know / not stated	5	10%

Source: Commission for Racial Equality – Race Relations Survey 2006.

Young, British Muslims 'getting more radical'

By Graeme Wilson, Political Correspondent

A bleak picture of a generation of young British Muslims radicalised by anti-Western views and misplaced multicultural policies is shown in a survey published today.

The study found disturbing evidence of young Muslims adopting more fundamentalist beliefs on key social and political issues than their parents or grandparents.

Forty per cent of Muslims between the ages of 16 and 24 said they would prefer to live under sharia law in Britain, a legal system based on the teachings of the Koran. The figure among over-55s, in contrast, was only 17 per cent.

> **'Unlike their parents, our young people feel that this is their country and are saying why are we being told we do not belong here'**

In some countries, people found guilty under sharia law face penalties such as beheading, stoning, the severing of a hand or being lashed.

The study, by the Right-wing think-tank Policy Exchange, also found a significant minority who expressed backing for Islamic terrorism.

One in eight young Muslims said they admired groups such as al-Qa'eda that 'are prepared to fight the West'.

Turning to issues of faith, 36 per cent of the young people questioned said they believed that a Muslim who converts to another religion should be 'punished by death'. Among the over-55s, the figure is only 19 per cent.

Three out of four young Muslims would prefer Muslim women to 'choose to wear the veil or hijab', compared to only a quarter of over-55s.

Support was also strong for Islamic schools, according to the Populus survey of 1,000 people commissioned by Policy Exchange.

Forty per cent of younger Muslims said they would want their children to attend an Islamic school, compared to only 20 per cent of over-55s.

Britain's foreign policies were a key issue among the Muslim population as a whole, with 58 per cent arguing that many of the world's problems are 'a result of arrogant Western attitudes'. However, knowledge of foreign affairs was sketchy, with only one in five knowing that Mahmoud Abbas was the Palestinian president.

The findings emerged as David Cameron, the Conservative leader, criticised the Government for trying to 'bully' immigrant communities into feeling British by telling them to run up the Union flag in their gardens or spy on their children.

But in a speech today, Mr Cameron will warn the Muslim community that it cannot use the 'screen of cultural sensitivity' to deny women their rights.

The Policy Exchange report, *Living Together Apart: British Muslims and the Paradox of Multiculturalism* says there is strong evidence of a 'growing religiosity' among young Muslims, with an increasing minority firmly rejecting Western life.

Munira Mirza, the broadcaster and one of the authors of the report, argued that multicultural policies pursued by the Government had succeeded in making things worse, rather than better.

She said: 'The emergence of a strong Muslim identity in Britain is, in part, a result of multi-cultural policies implemented since the 1980s which have emphasised difference at the expense of shared national identity and divided people along ethnic, religious and cultural lines.

'There is clearly a conflict within British Islam between a moderate majority that accepts the norms of British democracy and a growing minority that does not.'

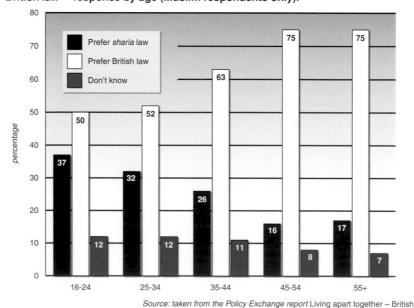

British Muslims and support for *sharia* law

'If I could choose, I would prefer to live in Britain under *sharia* law rather than British law' – response by age (Muslim respondents only).

Legend: Prefer *sharia* law (black); Prefer British law (white); Don't know (dark grey)

Age	Prefer sharia law	Prefer British law	Don't know
16-24	37	50	12
25-34	32	52	12
35-44	26	63	11
45-54	16	75	8
55+	17	75	7

Source: taken from the Policy Exchange report Living apart together – British Muslims and the paradox of multiculturalism. © *Policy Exchange 2007*

The report also raises questions about the scale of the problems created by Islamophobia, with 84 per cent of those questioned saying they believed they had been 'treated fairly' in Britain.

There was also criticism of the decision by some councils to ban Christian symbols in case they offended Muslims or other communities.

Three-quarters said it was wrong for a council to have banned an advert for a Christmas carol service.

Shahid Malik, the Muslim Labour MP for Dewsbury, said: 'This report makes very disturbing reading and it vindicates the concern many of us have that we're not doing enough to confront this issue.'

Baroness Uddin, the Muslim peer, said: 'Unlike their parents, our young people feel that this is their country and are saying why are we being told we do not belong here.

'There is also a problem of a lack of opportunities. Some people have been brutalised by their experiences with the police and this war on terror.'

In his speech in Birmingham today, Mr Cameron will criticise 'simplistic' attempts at community cohesion, such as Gordon Brown's call for people to put up the Union flag.

But he will also challenge elements of the Muslim community for denying women access to work, education, politics and even to mosques.

In a move that will please the Tory Right, Mr Cameron will warn that urgent action must be taken to get a grip of an immigration system that is out of control.

'It's the same whether it's the white grandmother worried about groups of asylum seekers or an unemployed Sikh youngster who sees eastern Europeans filling all the jobs.

'The Government needs to be in control of the situation. We can only live together if there is proper integration.

'And you can't have proper integration if people are coming into Britain at a faster rate than we can cope with.'

30 January 2007

The hijacking of British Islam

Executive summary of a report by Policy Exchange

'You will not find any confusion in which the Jews did not play a role…Their attempt at trying to immerse nations in vice and the spread of fornication. The Jews controlled this kind of trade and promoted it. They manage the bars in Europe and the United States and in Israel itself.'
Al-Hadith wa'l-thaqafa al-Islamiyya [Prophetic Tradition and Islamic Culture] – 1st Grade High School; found at the King Fahad Academy, west London.

'In the beginning of the twentieth century, a movement for the freedom of women was launched with the basic objective of driving women towards aberrant ways. This was patronised by Jews and Christians who made known that their ambition was to lead astray the aliens [sic].'
Women Who Deserve to go to Hell; found at the East London Mosque; and the Muslim Education Centre, High Wycombe.

'And if he apostatises after that, his head should be chopped off, according to the Hadith: **"Whoever changes his**

religion, kill him" [emphasis added].'
Fatawa Islamiyah – Islamic Verdicts, volume 5; found at the East London Mosque; the London Central Mosque and Islamic Centre (the 'Regent's Park Mosque').

'Whoever takes part in stoning a married adulterer, is rewarded for that, and it is not fitting for anyone to abstain from it if a ruling of stoning is issued.'
Fatawa Islamiyah – Islamic Verdicts, volume 6; found at the East London Mosque.

'Jihad against a tyrant, oppressors, people of bid'ah, or wrongdoers. This type of **Jihad is best done through force if possible** [emphasis added], otherwise, by tongue, or else by abhorring their deeds in one's heart.'

The Islamic Digest of Aqeedah and Fiqh [The Islamic Digest of Belief and Jurisprudence]; found at the Al-Muntada Al-Islami Trust, west London.

This report is the result of a year-long investigation carried out by Policy Exchange into the character of the literature currently available in mainstream sites of Islamic religious instruction in the UK.

During 2006 and 2007, four Muslim research teams travelled to towns and cities across the UK. They visited a large number of important Islamic religious institutions, including leading mosques, to determine the extent to which literature inculcating Muslim separatism and hatred of nonbelievers was accessible in those institutions – both in terms of being openly available and also being obtainable 'under the counter'. In total, almost 100 sites were visited.

This material was then passed to an expert academic authority, Denis MacEoin, who together with a team of independent experts, translated it (where necessary) and then analysed its content. The result is this report. It provides excerpts of that material in easily accessible, reference format offering a detailed compendium of exactly what was found and where. The texts presented here have been arranged according to the locations at which they were discovered. Some of them were available at multiple locations: that is why the reader will encounter several texts more than once. The end product is the most comprehensive academic survey of such literature ever produced in this country.

On the one hand, the results were reassuring: in only a minority of institutions – approximately 25% – was radical material found. What is more worrying is that these are among the best-funded and most dynamic institutions in Muslim Britain – some of which are held up as mainstream bodies. Many of the institutions featured here have been endowed with official recognition. This has come in the form of official visits from politicians and even members of the Royal Family; provision of funding; 'partnership' associations; or some other seal of approval.

Within the literature identified here, a number of key themes emerge – many of which focus around the twin concepts of 'loyalty' and 'enmity'. Simply put, these notions demand that the individual Muslim must not merely feel deep affection for and identity with his fellow believers and with all that is authentically Islamic. The individual Muslim must also feel an abhorrence for non-believers, hypocrites, heretics, and all that is deemed 'un-Islamic'. The latter category encompasses those Muslims who are judged to practise an insufficiently rigorous form of Islam. Much of the material is thus infused with a strident sectarianism, in which many Muslims – particularly the very large number of Sufis in this country and around the world – are placed beyond the pale.

More widely, Muslims are urged to separate themselves from people and things that are not considered Islamic; a separation that is to be mental, emotional, and at times, even physical. Western society, in particular, is held to be sinful, corros-ive and corrupting for Muslims. Western values – particularly concerning the position and rights of women and in the realm of sexuality generally – are rejected as inimical to Islam.

Hate and separatist literature is not the exclusive preserve of Muslims. On the contrary, offensive and troubling material is generated under the banner of most faiths

---

On occasion, this attitude of deep-rooted antipathy towards western society can descend into exhortations to violence and jihad against the 'enemies' of Islam. Such instances have been highlighted where they occur. Usually, the literature does not go that far, but is no less problematic for that. Without condoning or inciting terrorism, portions of it can sometimes provide a cultural hinterland – couched in religious terms – into which those who do encourage and conduct violence can move. They inculcate disgust for, and separation from, the unbelievers or 'kuffar', creating an ideological space which can be exploited by those who are prepared to justify and engage in terrorism against the West.

We recognise, of course, that hate and separatist literature is not the exclusive preserve of Muslims. On the contrary, offensive and troubling material is generated under the banner of most faiths. However, the hate and separatist literature found in some mosques and reported in these pages is of a wholly different order from that which one would expect to find in mainstream religious institutions of other faiths in this country today.

Adultery, apostasy and homosexuality, for instance, are deprecated by all the Abrahamic religions, and many others besides. But mainstream Christianity and Judaism, at least as practised in western Europe today, do not respond to these spiritual challenges with either an implied or an explicit threat of violence; nor do they seek to place the blame for developments such as birth control on dark conspiratorial forces (such as the notion that contraception is a plot to keep Muslim populations low).

Beyond the character of the literature under focus here, the report also exposes some of the forces vying for control of Britain's mosques: the Jamaat-e-Islami, the Deobandis and, in particular, the Wahhabites. With regard to the latter, it is clear that the influence of Saudi Arabia is both powerful and malign. Much of the material featured here is connected in some way with the Saudi Kingdom – whether by virtue of being written by members of the Wahhabite religious establishment; being published and distributed by official, or semi-official Saudi institutions; or being found in Saudi-funded, or linked, mosques and schools in this country. For this reason, the report argues, there needs now to be a proper audit of the costs and benefits of the Saudi-UK relationship.
October 2007

⇨ The above information is reprinted with kind permission from Policy Exchange, an independent think tank. Visit www.policyexchange.org. uk for more information.
© *Policy Exchange*

Among other locations, hate literature was allegedly found at the East London Mosque

Race relations 2006

Information from Ipsos MORI

Despite ongoing issues relating to the 2005 London bombings, the threat of terrorism and the impact of new immigrants to the country, people's own experiences of prejudice and discrimination appear relatively unchanged from previous years. Perceptions of integration and attitudes to race relations also remain the same with ethnic minorities continuing the trend of being more positive than white people on most measures.

The qualitative research finds that people feel meaningful social interaction between different ethnic groups would be better at fostering a shared sense of Britishness and good race relations than more formal or compulsory means like citizenship classes or English language lessons. The survey data also support this notion: people who mix both within the context of work, school and college and in more social situations are among the most positive about diversity and integration while people who only mix at work, school and college are considerably less so. This highlights that it is not just social interaction which is important, but that the nature of interactions between people from different ethnic groups also plays a role.

Ethnic minorities tend to mix more than white people, although this most likely reflects the fact that as minority groups they have more opportunity to mix with white people than vice versa. There do, however, appear to be some key differences within ethnic minority communities with black people generally reporting that they mix more regularly than Asian people, reflecting trends recorded in the National Citizenship Survey.

Technical details

1,068 British adults, aged 16+ were interviewed face-to-face in home between 28 September and 3 October 2006. 223 ethnic minority adults from black and Asian ethnic groups aged 16+ were interviewed in-street across England between 15 and 20 November 2006. Data in both the ethnic minority and general public samples are weighted to the known national profiles. Four discussion groups were conducted across London (2 groups), Birmingham (1 group) and Edinburgh (1 group) between 10 and 12 October 2006.
27 November 2006

⇨ The above information is reprinted with kind permission from Ipsos MORI, the UK research company. Visit www.ipsos-mori.com for more information.

© Ipsos MORI

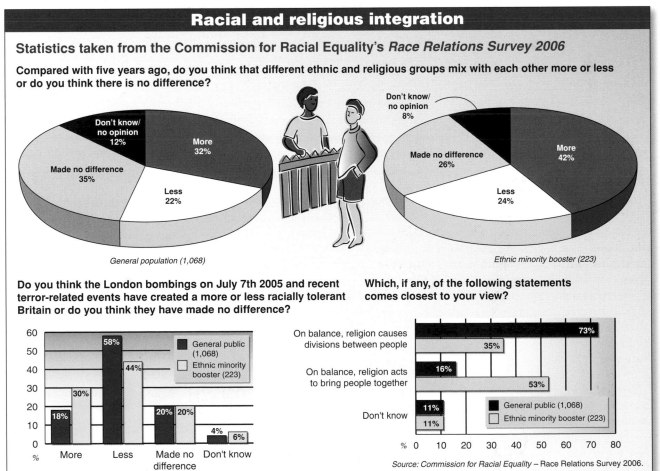

Racial and religious integration

Statistics taken from the Commission for Racial Equality's *Race Relations Survey 2006*

Compared with five years ago, do you think that different ethnic and religious groups mix with each other more or less or do you think there is no difference?

General population (1,068):
- Don't know/no opinion 12%
- More 32%
- Less 22%
- Made no difference 35%

Ethnic minority booster (223):
- Don't know/no opinion 8%
- More 42%
- Less 24%
- Made no difference 26%

Do you think the London bombings on July 7th 2005 and recent terror-related events have created a more or less racially tolerant Britain or do you think they have made no difference?

	General public (1,068)	Ethnic minority booster (223)
More	18%	30%
Less	58%	44%
Made no difference	20%	20%
Don't know	4%	6%

Which, if any, of the following statements comes closest to your view?

	General public (1,068)	Ethnic minority booster (223)
On balance, religion causes divisions between people	73%	35%
On balance, religion acts to bring people together	16%	53%
Don't know	11%	11%

Source: Commission for Racial Equality – Race Relations Survey 2006.

Public turns on animal terrorists

By Philip Johnston,
Home Affairs Editor

Extremist behaviour by animal rights protesters has had the effect of increasing public support for testing new medical treatments on animals, a poll for the *Daily Telegraph* has found.

The proportion of people who approve of animal testing is now at an all-time high and more than three-quarters believe that the more fanatical activists can justifiably be defined as 'terrorists'.

High-profile campaigns, such as intimidating scientists and threatening shareholders in pharmaceutical companies, appear to have backfired badly.

The YouGov survey suggests that fewer than one person in five considers animal testing to be unacceptable in any circumstance.

More than 70 per cent said they accepted that experimentation on animals was sometimes essential because alternative methods were unavailable.

There was also widespread concern that a ban on medical research on animals would merely encourage pharmaceutical multinationals to set up abroad, where the safeguards that exist in Britain against causing unnecessary suffering may be absent.

The findings appear to contradict the claims often made by opponents of animal testing that there is 'overwhelming' public support for their cause. While people might prefer not to see animals suffer, just 19 per cent took the view that alternative methods of testing were always available.

Brian Cass, the managing director of Huntingdon Life Sciences, an animal-testing research company which has been the target of activists for several years, said: 'The issue has had so much publicity that organisations like ourselves have gone out of our way to provide an almost open laboratory to the media.

'This has brought a much more open presentation of both how animal testing is done and the legal requirements that control it. Once people understand what is going on they are in a much better position to form objective judgements. When they do so they tend to support the work.'

Previous polls have shown opinion more or less evenly divided on animal testing.

YouGov's findings indicate that by stepping up their campaign, extremists have damaged their cause. While most people have no objection to campaigners staging peaceful demonstrations, they draw the line at some of the activities seen in recent years.

There was strong support for the 12-year jail terms given this month to three extremists who had been involved in a campaign of intimidation, including the disinterment of the body of a woman whose family bred animals for experimentation.

Opposition to threats, hate campaigns and vandalism is almost universal and 88 per cent believe it is wrong to post the names and addresses of people connected with animal testing on the internet.

Alistair Currie, the campaigns director of the British Union for the Abolition of Vivisection, said extremists had not helped the animal rights cause.

'It has produced an image problem for the animal rights movement as a whole,' he said. 'But that doesn't necessarily mean people are more committed to animal experiments than they were previously.'

The findings suggest that Tony Blair was very much in tune with public opinion when he took the unusual step of agreeing to sign a petition affirming support for the right of scientists to conduct legitimate animal experiments.

He also said that the Government would consider a new law to protect the identities of those involved in testing.

His move came amid continuing protests in Oxford against plans for a new medical research laboratory at the university and complaints that despite a few high-profile prosecutions, the police are not doing enough to disrupt the activities of known extremists.

Part of the reason for changing public attitudes could be an appreciation that animals are no longer used to test cosmetics in Britain, though the number of tests for medical purposes is rising. In 2004, there were around 2.85 million 'procedures', a rise of just over two per cent on the previous year.
30 May 2006
© Telegraph Group Limited, London 2006

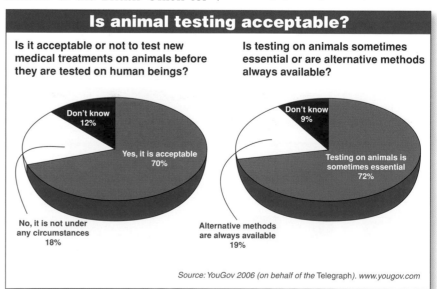

Is animal testing acceptable?

Is it acceptable or not to test new medical treatments on animals before they are tested on human beings?

- Don't know 12%
- Yes, it is acceptable 70%
- No, it is not under any circumstances 18%

Is testing on animals sometimes essential or are alternative methods always available?

- Don't know 9%
- Testing on animals is sometimes essential 72%
- Alternative methods are always available 19%

Source: YouGov 2006 (on behalf of the Telegraph*). www.yougov.com*

Animal rights terrorism is on the increase

And animal rights activists aren't doing enough to stop it

By Wesley J. Smith

Terrorism takes many forms. Recently, animal rights terrorists have unleashed an organised campaign of violence and intimidation against animal industries and their service companies – such as banks, auditing companies, and insurance brokers.

A pattern has developed: websites identify people to be terrorised because of their involvement with animal-using industries; these sites list their personal information, including home addresses, phone numbers, Social Security numbers, even the names, ages, and schools of their children. Militants use this information to send anonymous death threats to the children of targets, backed by mailed video tapes of their family members. They steal mail, shatter windows while the family is home, burn cars, make false bomb threats, cover homes with graffiti, take out subscriptions to pornographic magazines in the name of the target, steal identities, and otherwise ruin their victims' lives.

One of the most active of these groups is Stop Huntingdon Animal Cruelty (SHAC), which is dedicated to driving Huntingdon Life Sciences (HLS) out of business because it tests drugs on animals. As William Trundley, the vice president for Corporate Security & Investigations

> **Recently, animal rights terrorists have unleashed an organised campaign of violence and intimidation against animal industries and their service companies**

at GlaxoSmithKline, recently testified, SHAC members distribute a 'SHAC Terror Card' to potential victims, which reads:

'Do you do business with Huntingdon Life Sciences? . . . If you do, there's something you should know . . . Radical animal rights activists have been targeting executives and employees of companies that work with HLS, with criminal activity including: smashed windows; spray painted houses; glued locks; vandalised cars; stolen credit card numbers; ID theft; fraud; and continuous acts of harassment and intimidation against employees, their children and spouses.'

The card states that 'the only way to end or prevent such attacks . . . is to stop doing business with Huntingdon.'

SHAC has grown so brazen that it demands that when targeted companies capitulate to its demands, they do so publicly. The SHAC website instructs:

'To all suppliers: If you have severed your links with Huntingdon Life Sciences, please let the campaign know. You can send a simple email to info@shac.net stating the following: " . . . . . . (name of your company) have severed their links with HLS and terminated their contract, and will not be dealing with them now or in the future, directly or indirectly." This will enable supporters to be kept up to date with which companies are still involved with Huntingdon Life Sciences.'

This is terrorism, pure and simple – and unfortunately, it's working. SHAC and its allies, such as the Animal Liberation Front, have scared a number of businesses into cutting ties with Huntingdon Life Sciences, including the huge auditing firm of Deloitte & Touche. At present, SHAC's website lists 113 companies that have complied with its demands, including Johnson & Johnson, Washington Mutual, UBS Global Capital, Nucryst Pharmaceutical, and Chubb.

The site also crows about its most recent triumph: the submission of the New York Stock Exchange to animal liberationist demands. In 2005, the NYSE unexpectedly reversed a decision to list Huntingdon Life Sciences, on the morning the listing was to commence. Big Board executives refused to either explain

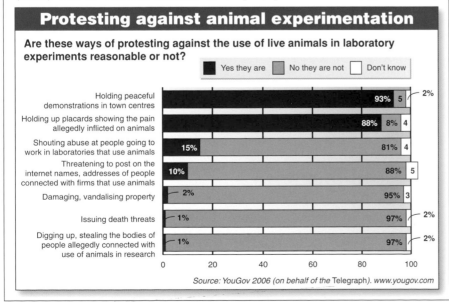

Protesting against animal experimentation

Are these ways of protesting against the use of live animals in laboratory experiments reasonable or not?

Legend: ■ Yes they are ▨ No they are not □ Don't know

	Yes they are	No they are not	Don't know
Holding peaceful demonstrations in town centres	93%	5	2%
Holding up placards showing the pain allegedly inflicted on animals	88%	8%	4
Shouting abuse at people going to work in laboratories that use animals	15%	81%	4
Threatening to post on the internet names, addresses of people connected with firms that use animals	10%	88%	5
Damaging, vandalising property	2%	95%	3
Issuing death threats	1%	97%	2%
Digging up, stealing the bodies of people allegedly connected with use of animals in research	1%	97%	2%

Axis: 0 20 40 60 80 100

Source: YouGov 2006 (on behalf of the Telegraph). www.yougov.com

or justify their decision – even to a United States Senate committee. The rescission came immediately after liberationists vandalised an executive's yacht club and threatened to target Exchange employees.

Now the *Telegraph* reports that UK animal liberationists plan to hold a 'training camp' to 'export terror' throughout Europe this June. 'The AR 2006 camp', will 'feature classes in potentially lethal physical techniques . . . that could be used against security guards at pharmaceutical companies and huntsmen.'

Law enforcement is on heightened alert to protect against animal rights terrorism, and legislation (H.R. 4239) is wending its way through the House of Representatives to make such lawlessness more easily prosecuted. These are necessary steps. But given the ideological zealotry of these extremists, the best chance we have of stopping the violence is for fellow believers to convince the terrorists among them to stay within the law.

But so far, the 'mainstream' leadership of the animal rights movement has generally failed to do so. They have been mostly silent, at times ambivalent, and in a few cases, even supportive. The People for the Ethical Treatment of Animals (PETA), for example, refuses to condemn arson and vandalism in the name of animal liberation and likens such crimes to the French Resistance and the Underground Railroad. PETA's second in command, Bruce Friedrich, sure seemed to support violence when he told an animal liberation conference in 2001:

'Of course, we're going to be as a movement blowing stuff up and smashing windows. For the record, I don't do this stuff, but I do advocate it. I think it is a great way to bring about animal liberation. And considering the level of the atrocity and the level of the suffering, I think it would be a great thing if all of these fast food outlets and slaughter houses and laboratories – and the banks that fund them – exploded tomorrow.'

From time to time, an animal rights activist will speak up. Princeton's Peter Singer, the godfather of animal liberation, occasionally takes a mild line against using violence and threats in the name of animal rights, as he did, for example, in 'Humans are Sentient Too.' But even here, Singer mostly punted, asserting that beyond expressing their genuine disapproval, 'There is little more that the non-violent majority of the animal movement can do. The next step is really up to the government and the research community.'

Surely there is more to be done than the wagging of fingers. If animal rights terror continues to be ratcheted up, someone is going to be killed. If that happens, those who winked at violence in the name of saving the animals will wish they had instead insisted to the terrorists among them: 'Not in our name.'

Wesley J. Smith is a senior fellow at the Discovery Institute and a consultant for the Center for Bioethics and Culture.
26 May 2006

⇨ The above information is reprinted with kind permission from the US news and opinions website the Daily Standard. Visit www.weeklystandard.com for more information.

© *Daily Standard*

The truth about 'animal rights terrorism'

Statistics reveal that it consists of rare and mostly minor incidents carried out by a handful of losers. So why is everyone so obsessed with it?

The extremists' heyday is over

For all the present handwringing over animal rights extremism and terrorism, the heyday of such activities was in the mid-Eighties to the mid-Nineties. It's notoriously difficult to get facts and figures about the number and size of violent actions by animal rights activists over the past 20 years; such things only started to be seriously measured, by the Association of the British Pharmaceutical Industry, in 2002. However, it is broadly accepted that the 'high point' for animal rights extremism – certainly in terms of violence and media stunts – occurred between 1985 and 1995. Since then, animal rights groups have largely engaged in small protests outside individuals' homes or workplaces and in occasional acts of arson or intimidation.

The Animal Liberation Front (ALF) was founded in 1976, and the Animal Rights Militia in 1985 – both groups are said to have used violence, though the ALF claims that it does not support violence against people. For all the hysterical arguments about an Afghan-style network of animal rights extremists in Britain, even the ALF, the most notorious group, does not have a centralised structure with a leadership or 'troops'. Rather, it is pretty much a media organisation, consisting mainly of a website and a press office that publicises the usually small-scale actions of various 'freelancers' who support the ALF. As the pro-research group the Research Defence Society says, 'The ALF has never been an organisation with members and a constitution: it is a badge of convenience. Extremists carry out actions in its name, or in the name of other, similarly unstructured groups'.

In the period from 1985 to 1995, some animal rights extremists actually detonated a few high explosive devices, which they no longer do today. In the 1980s there was a sporadic bombing campaign,

Support for animal testers

Pharmaceutical companies say they would transfer their research facilities abroad if they were banned from using animals in medical research in this country or the rules on their use were tightened significantly. Do you think the companies are bluffing or not?

What would be your reaction if they did move their research facilities abroad?

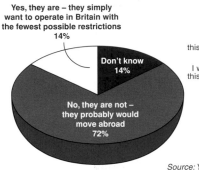

Yes, they are – they simply want to operate in Britain with the fewest possible restrictions 14%

Don't know 14%

No, they are not – they probably would move abroad 72%

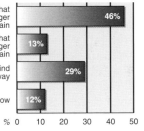

I would be sorry that this work were no longer being done in Britain — 46%

I would be pleased that this work were no longer being done in Britain — 13%

I would not mind either way — 29%

Don't know — 12%

% 0 10 20 30 40 50

Source: YouGov 2006 (on behalf of the Telegraph). www.yougov.com

in which letter bombs and firebombs were directed against leading scientists and some politicians. No one was killed or seriously injured in that campaign. The period of 1989/1990 was the first and last time that activists used high explosives. They blew up Senate House at Bristol University (in the middle of the night when it was empty) in February 1989 using plastic explosives; in May 1990 they planted plastic explosive devices under the cars of two scientists in the West Country, both of which exploded but without injuring the scientists.

In 1993/1994, there was a campaign of sending dangerous postal devices to scientists, including mousetraps primed with razor blades in padded envelopes, small explosives in parcels, and also hoax bombs. By the middle of 1994, 100 such devices had been sent. Again there were no fatalities or serious injuries. A group called the Justice Department claimed responsibility for the postal campaign, and the activists responsible were all eventually caught, charged and given lengthy prison sentences.

Alongside these violent tactics, some activists executed headline-grabbing stunts, including the infamous contamination scares. In the late Eighties there was the Mars Bar Hoax, when animal rights activists led Mars to believe that some of its stock had been poisoned in protest at the use of monkeys in tooth-decay experiments. The withdrawal of stock and bad publicity

cost Mars an estimated £3million in lost sales. Similar contamination hoaxes were played on Lucozade and L'Oreal.

Even during this 'heyday', animal rights extremists hardly posed a great threat. These were handfuls of individuals, sometimes even loners, who decided to do something shocking and outrageous in the name of those 'badges of convenience' the ALF or the Animal Rights Militia, or perhaps in the name of their own fancily-titled group that they conjured up while sitting at home. So when those behind the postal-device campaign in 1993/1994 were banged up, such methods of intimidation came to a halt – there was no movement or group of comrades to continue the campaign, which had been the work of some cranky individuals.

After 1994, there was a notable decline in violent tactics among animal rights activists, who instead focused their energies on protesting outside homes or research laboratories, sending menacing letters to or intimidating scientists and their supporters, and occasionally smashing windows and damaging cars. In 2001, Brian Cass, MD of the medical research company Huntingdon Life Sciences, was savagely beaten by three activists with baseball bats – an incident which stands out because, today, it is quite rare for activists to use such naked violence.

Yet despite the general decline in bombings and big media stunts,

there seems to be greater political and cultural concern, from the top of the government down, with 'animal rights terrorism' today than there was in 1985-1995, when there actually existed something approximating animal rights terrorism. This would suggest that there is something more to today's constant demands for clampdowns on the 'extremists' and 'terrorists' than the facts and figures relating to their activities.

After 1994, there was a notable decline in violent tactics among animal rights activists

---

The truth about today's 'extremist incidents'

Today, you will sometimes read newspaper articles which say there are still, 10 years after the heyday ended, hundreds of animal rights 'extremist incidents' every year in the UK. Yet if you break the figures down, you'll see that most of these incidents are small-scale, sometimes even insignificant; they could not seriously be defined as terrorism.

Since 2002, the Association of the British Pharmaceutical Industry (ABPI) has been collating figures relating to animal rights activism. Most of the media coverage on the number of activities is based on these figures. Yet the media's interpretation can sometimes be misleading. For example, one report claimed that in 2005 there were 'around 1,500 animal rights incidents'. It is true that the ABPI report shows around 1,500 'incidents' in that year, but its clear and uncomplicated figures show that the vast majority of those incidents were demonstrations. Out of 1,508 incidents, 1,205 were demonstrations.

Likewise, of 1,692 incidents in 2004, 1,077 were demonstrations; of 1,414 incidents in 2003, 914 were demonstrations; and of 1,115 incidents in 2002, 830 were demonstrations. The average number of demonstrators at these events in each year shows up how pathetic these collections of activists are. In 2002, there was an average of 13.9

demonstrators at each demo; in 2003 that fell to an average of 12.5; it fell again in 2004, to an average of 10.1, and again in 2005 to an average of 8.9.

No doubt some of these demos were irritating. According to the ABPI, 'Nearly all demonstrations are accompanied by noise, for example with megaphones and drums, and are usually intimidating in nature.' But extremism? Terrorism? It doesn't seem so. And if we are going to problematise all demonstrations that are noisy, or even 'intimidating in nature', that is a recipe for further restricting the right to protest in Britain. It is in the nature of protesting to be loud, sometimes even obnoxious.

Despite the general decline in bombings and big media stunts, there seems to be greater political and cultural concern . . . with 'animal rights terrorism' today than there was in 1985-1995

Leaving aside protests, some animal rights activists do engage in cowardly acts of intimidation. But the number of such acts remains fairly low and it seems to be falling. If you exclude protests from the list of animal rights incidents between 2002 and 2005, there are also the following categories:

Abusive or threatening letters or text messages

These tend to fluctuate. There were 23 such incidents in 2002, 38 in 2003 and then a big rise to 108 in 2004; however, they fell to 36 in 2005. No doubt such letters and text messages can be distressing for those who receive them, but the numbers are quite small. For example, there were fewer threatening letters or texts in the 2002/2003 period (61) than there were dangerous postal devices in the earlier 1993/1994 period (over 100).

Blockades

This is when activists block the entrance to a research facility or breeding farm: there were three blockades in 2002 and four in 2003, but none in 2004 or 2005.

Phone, fax, email blockade

Again, the number of these tends to fluctuate. There were 21 in 2002, 40 in 2003, 37 in 2004, but only eight in 2005.

Fireworks (large, targeted at private residences)

This rather peculiar category, where activists fire fireworks into the gardens or against the windows of researchers' and others' homes, seems to have been popular in 2002, but no longer. There were 34 such incidents in 2002, 12 in 2003, but none in 2004 or 2005.

Damage to company, personal and public property

This illegal activity can include everything from usually small-scale acts of arson to the smashing of windows or the damaging of cars. Often it comes across more like the work of overgrown teenagers than serious terrorists. In 2002 there were 60 such incidents; in 2003 there were 146; in 2004 there were 177; and in 2005 there were 85.

Intimidation

In terms of potentially the most distressing animal rights activity, where they harass those who work in or around medical research, there has been a steady decline over the past two years. In 2002 there were 135 'home visits', where activists go to the home of a worker, usually in the middle of the night, and make noise or leave a threatening note of some sort; in 2003 there were 259 home visits; in 2004 there were 179; in 2005 there were 57. The ABPI announced just last month that for the first six months of 2006 home visits have, again, 'declined dramatically to just 15 – under half the number in the same period last year and 14 per cent of the total for the first six months of 2004'. The ABPI figures also contain the category 'Personal attack, slight injury': there were seven incidents in 2002, one in 2003, none in 2004, and six in 2005.

What kind of 'terrorists' cause between zero and seven 'slight injuries' in any given year? Or fire fireworks rather than missiles? Or

send abusive letters rather than letters with bladed-mousetraps in them, as animal rights activists did in the past? A closer look at the facts and figures behind animal rights activities suggests they tend to be small-scale, sporadic and still quite rare. They also show that such activists are becoming more and more isolated and opportunistic. With increased security and surveillance at research labs, following the activities of 1985-1995, activists are increasingly forced to chuck firecrackers into individuals' gardens, or send them rude texts, or shout outside their home at 1am in the morning. No doubt this is distressing for some of those on the receiving end, who should take whatever measures they deem necessary to get these brattish misanthropes off their property. But it does not add up to 'terrorism', or even very much 'extremism' – certainly not of the variety that requires a big debate between Bush and Blair or specific new sections of legislation to deal with it.

Where animal rights activists occasionally break the law and harass or intimidate individuals, the police should deal with it. But to call for heavy-handed 'anti-terror' measures to sort them out is not only an overreaction – it is also a demand for the law to fight our battles for us, as if the arguments and the protests of these animal rights activists are too scary and dangerous to face down by ourselves. Do we have such little conviction in the rightness of animal research and scientific endeavour?

Conclusion

Animal rights activists or extremists are not the biggest threat to medical research. They are not leading a charge against science and progress. On the contrary, it would be more accurate to say that they are parasitical on a broader doubt and suspicion that exists today about the work of scientists, and the idea that humans should intervene in nature, push science forward, and 'play God'. Obsessing over these individuals is a massive displacement activity. Rather than address the cause of today's anti-science sentiment, too many people are trying to clamp down on the most degraded symptom of the sentiment: activists who believe that rats and dogs and humans are all pretty much the same.

These small groups feed off a top-down uncertainty about animal testing, and scientific inquiry itself. The reason they have been able to dominate the debate about animal research in recent years is not because they are strong or powerful or especially disruptive; indeed, all the evidence suggests that their numbers are becoming smaller and their actions less threatening and, if the Hammond body theft and the attack on the pro-hunting grandmother are any indication, more self-destructively erratic. Rather, animal rights activists and protesters sound loud only because everyone else has remained so quiet.

Consider the issue of primate experimentation. It is widely assumed that the reason why Cambridge University shelved, in January 2004, its plans to build a world-class primate research centre is because of the antics of animal rights activists. No doubt the activists' constant protesting and threats had an impact on those involved in the project, from the builders to the scientists. But it is much more likely to have been official dithering about the worth of primate research that put paid to the Cambridge project. The government failed publicly to support the research institution until it was too late; research on great apes (chimps, gorillas and orang-utans) was banned in 1986, under the Animals (Scientific Procedures) Act; and the Animals Procedure Committee,

which advises the home secretary on matters relating to the Animals Act, says it has the goal of 'minimising and eventually eliminating primate use and suffering'. So presumably it was opposed to, or at least uncertain about, the building of the Cambridge facility.

This is the real problem: not a handful of big-mouthed animal-lovers in anoraks, or scary 'terrorists' with imaginary bombs, but a defensiveness about research at the heart of government and the scientific establishment itself. Such equivocation effectively gives a green light to animal rights activists to continue shouting about the allegedly dodgy things going on inside labs and research facilities, and to harass those who work on them. After all, if society is red-faced about something like primate research, declaring that its ultimate aim is to wind it down, then what is to stop activists from loudly demanding that it be banned right now? Officialdom's unwillingness to stand up and defend

the important work of medical researchers effectively makes such workers fair game for the attentions of anti-science elements.

Now, the government and its supporters are trying to do with heavy-handed laws what they have failed to do with words and actions – defend medical research. Unable to articulate the argument for such research in any meaningful way the government chooses to chase after a bunch of no-mark animal rights activists instead. But the best way to stop animal rights activism is to defend, loudly and proudly, the work of animal researchers – and to stop depicting some disgruntled losers as a terrible and evil threat.

10 August 2006

⇨ The above information is reprinted with kind permission from Spiked and is extracted from an article by Brendan O'Neill. Visit www.spiked-online.com to view the full text and references or for more information.

© *Spiked*

Attitudes to animal rights activists

Three animal rights activists were sentenced to 12 years in prison recently for making death threats, planting bombs, vandalising property and digging up someone's remains from a church graveyard. How do you feel about their 12-year sentence?

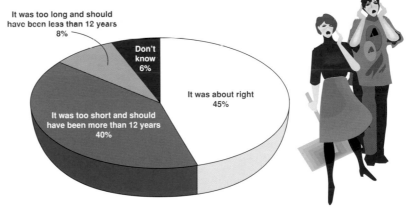

It was too long and should have been less than 12 years
8%

Don't know
6%

It was about right
45%

It was too short and should have been more than 12 years
40%

Is it fair to call people who behave like these animal rights activists 'terrorists' or not?

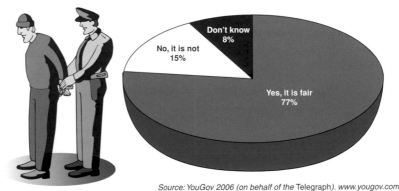

Don't know
8%

No, it is not
15%

Yes, it is fair
77%

Source: YouGov 2006 (on behalf of the Telegraph*). www.yougov.com*

How do we counter terrorism?

Information from Theos

By Francis Murphy

The terrorists responsible for the failed attacks in London and Glasgow may not have claimed any lives, but they did claim reputations. Theos' recent research into the attempts' effects on public perception shows that their actions were not without negative consequences. 71% of those questioned thought the events to have given Islam a bad name, while 54% felt the standing of religion in general to have suffered.

Can we judge a whole religion – or even religion generally – by the actions of a few adherents?

The findings come on the back of an announcement that Gordon Brown's cabinet will no longer refer to the Islamic religion in connection with terrorism. Gone too is the controversial 'War on Terror' label, which occasioned so much comment when it was first adopted by Brown's predecessor. As the new PM looks to redefine the terms of the debate so as to avoid stoking community divisions – part of a broader agenda which has also seen the revival of traditional symbols of British unity – Theos' research raises some important questions about how we engage as a society with religions and the terrorists who invoke them.

Can we judge a whole religion – or even religion generally – by the actions of a few adherents? That nearly three-quarters of the public feel Islam to have been given a bad name

by the failed bombings indicates that many of us are willing to do so. It was perhaps in recognition of this that British Muslims felt the need to stage an anti-terror rally in Glasgow, and to take out full-page advertisements in the national press declaring that such attacks are not in their name. But why should a law-abiding Muslim feel he or she has to answer for the actions of those who find in faith a justification for terror?

Part of the problem may be the theological illiteracy of the debate which surrounds such episodes. The ideas which motivate atrocities are often left unanalysed. Recourse is instead made to crude reductionism: there is a tacit assumption in much of the reportage that religious rhetoric must necessarily be acting as a primitive mask for something else, such as socio-economic concerns or foreign policy objections. Perhaps

if British Muslims were understood more in terms of the teachings to which they subscribe, rather than as a homogeneous community given to expressing its grievances in 'God-talk', it would be easier to distinguish between competing accounts of Muslim teaching and to identify the character of those which encourage violence. Muslims might begin to see how to combat extremists on their own territory, while the non-Muslim majority would avoid giving the impression of indiscriminate suspicion.

That over half of respondents thought the reputation of religion generally to have suffered in the wake of the events which occurred in London and Glasgow serves to underline the point: theological ignorance is widespread. We would not consider it a sign of nuanced thinking if a man were to dislike all forms of human government in view of the crimes of Pol Pot and Stalin, and it does not say much for the

popular understanding of religion if Zoroastrianism and Unitarianism are thought to have been tarnished by Wahhabist outrages. Recent atheist apologias by people who should know better have manifested a similar lack of discernment, condemning a monolithic 'religion' which has no real-life equivalent. A more reflective discourse – making distinctions where they exist – is needed. And we must be willing to engage with and critique destructive theologies on their own terms.

Why should a law-abiding Muslim feel he or she has to answer for the actions of those who find in faith a justification for terror?

This is not to say that direct engagement with religious motivations will always result in welcome conclusions. In a recent piece for the *International Herald Tribune* ('Only traditional Islam can do it', 8th July 2007) theologians Phillip Blond and Adrian Pabst observe that 'the Koran contains clear and lethal injunctions against apostates, idolaters and those who challenge Muslim territorial ascendancy'; even as they argue that recent 'Islamic terrorism' owes little to classical Islam itself, the authors contend that the Muslim religion's foundational text endorses certain forms of violence. Some Muslims would doubtless disagree with Pabst and Blond's reading of the Koran, and there is clearly scope for debate. But the debate should be had. Honest engagement will demand the asking of tougher questions than those to which our political class has been accustomed until now.

There will be those who say that these are long-term concerns, and that theological discussion – with its ivory tower connotations – will do little to overcome present hostilities. Yet Theos' research would seem to suggest that the question is not going to go away any time soon. If the new prime minister's concern for national unity is truly forward-looking, he

should be struck by the fact that the youngest class of respondents (18-25) were more than twice as likely as those over 65 to regard Islam as 'fundamentally a religion of war'.

If we truly want to counter terrorism, we need to start doing some theology.

Francis Murphy is a postgraduate student of theology at Oxford.
12 July 2006

⇨ Information from Theos, the public theology think tank. Visit www.theosthinktank.co.uk for more.
© Theos

Terrorism Act 2006

Information from the Home Office

The Terrorism Act contains a comprehensive package of measures designed to ensure that the police, intelligence agencies and courts have all the tools they require to tackle terrorism and bring perpetrators to justice.

The Act received Royal Assent on 30 March 2006. This Act was not a direct response to the July attacks on London as new terrorism legislation had already been planned.

After the attacks, however, we consulted with law enforcement and intelligence agencies, to make sure that their views were considered when we developed the legislation.

Content of the Terrorism Act

The Terrorism Act specifically aims to make it more difficult for extremists to abuse the freedoms we cherish, in order to encourage others to commit terrorist acts.

The Act creates a number of new offences. Once it is brought into force, it will be a criminal offence to commit:

⇨ Acts Preparatory to Terrorism – This aims to capture those planning serious acts of terrorism.

⇨ Encouragement to Terrorism – This makes it a criminal offence to directly or indirectly incite or encourage others to commit acts of terrorism. This will include the glorification of terrorism, where this may be understood as encouraging the emulation of terrorism.

⇨ Dissemination of Terrorist Publications – This will cover the sale, loan, or other dissemination of terrorist publications. This will include those publications that encourage terrorism, and those that provide assistance to terrorists.

⇨ Terrorist training offences – This makes sure that anyone who gives or receives training in terrorist techniques can be prosecuted. The Act also criminalises attendance at a place of terrorist training.

The Act also makes amendments to existing legislation, including:

⇨ Introducing warrants to enable the police to search any property owned or controlled by a terrorist suspect.

⇨ Extending terrorism stop and search powers to cover bays and estuaries.

⇨ Extending police powers to detain suspects after arrest for up to 28 days (though periods of more than two days must be approved by a judicial authority).

⇨ Improved search powers at ports.

⇨ Increased flexibility of the proscription regime, including the power to proscribe groups that glorify terrorism.

⇨ The above information is reprinted with kind permission from the Home Office. Visit www.homeoffice.gov.uk for more information.
© Crown copyright

Counter-terrorism strategy

Information from the Home Office

About the counter-terrorism strategy

The key aim of the counter-terrorism strategy is to reduce the risk from international terrorism so that people can go about their business freely and with confidence.

Who is involved?

Developing and delivering the government's counter-terrorism strategy involves stakeholders from across government departments, the emergency services, voluntary organisations, the business sector and partners from across the world.

What is the strategy based on?

Since early 2003, the United Kingdom has had a long-term strategy for countering international terrorism (known within government as CONTEST). Its aim is to reduce the risk from international terrorism, so that people can go about their daily lives freely and with confidence. The strategy is divided into four principal strands: Prevent, Pursue, Protect and Prepare.

Prevent

The Prevent strand is concerned with tackling the radicalisation of individuals, both in the UK and elsewhere, which sustains the international terrorist threat. The government seek to do this by:

⇨ tackling disadvantage and supporting reform by addressing structural problems in the UK and overseas that may contribute to radicalisation, such as inequalities and discrimination;

⇨ deterring those who facilitate terrorism and those who encourage others to become terrorists by changing the environment in which the extremists and those radicalising others can operate;

The key aim of the counter-terrorism strategy is to reduce the risk from international terrorism so that people can go about their business freely and with confidence

---

⇨ engaging in the battle of ideas by challenging the ideologies that extremists believe can justify the use of violence, primarily by helping Muslims who wish to dispute these ideas to do so.

Pursue

The Pursue strand is concerned with reducing the terrorist threat to the UK and to UK interests overseas by disrupting terrorists and their operations. It has a number of aspects:

⇨ gathering intelligence and improving our ability to identify and understand the terrorist threat;

⇨ disrupting terrorist activity and taking action to frustrate

terrorist attacks and to bring terrorists to justice through prosecution and other means, including strengthening the legal framework against terrorism;

⇨ international co-operation by working with partners and allies overseas to strengthen our intelligence effort and achieve disruption of terrorists outside the UK.

Protect

The Protect strand is concerned with reducing the vulnerability of the UK and UK interests overseas to a terrorist attack. This covers a range of issues including:

⇨ strengthening border security, so that terrorists and those who inspire them can be prevented from travelling here and we can get better intelligence about suspects who travel, including improving our identity management;

⇨ protecting key utilities by working with the private sector;

⇨ transport; reducing the risk and impact of attacks through security and technological advances;

⇨ crowded places; protecting people going about their daily lives.

Prepare

The Prepare strand is concerned with ensuring that the UK is as ready as it can be for the consequences of a terrorist attack. The key elements are:

⇨ identifying the potential risks the UK faces from terrorism and assessing their impact;

⇨ building the necessary capabilities to respond to attacks;

⇨ continually evaluating and testing our preparedness, including through identifying lessons from exercises and real-life events.

Targeting terrorist funds

Money underpins all terrorist activity – without it there can be no attacks and, more fundamentally, no training, recruitment, facilitation or welfare support for terrorist groups.

The disruption of terrorist financing is a key element of the government's overall fight against terrorism, involving close working across government between the intelligence and law enforcement agencies and the financial sector.

This work aims to create a hostile environment for terrorists by disrupting and cutting off their funds in order to deter them from using financial systems to further their work.

The UK is at the forefront of international activity in this area, and working closely with governments in other nations.

Goals of the counter-terrorist finance strategy

The main goals of the government's strategy are:
⇨ to decrease the amount of funds raised in the UK for terrorist purposes by creating as hostile an environment as possible;
⇨ to identify and disrupt terrorist facilitators, and stop the flow of funds overseas where they impact on UK interests;
⇨ to encourage and assist other countries in enhancing their own capabilities against terrorist finance.

There are a number of ways to challenge terrorist fundraising. For example, the UK's terrorist asset freezing powers publicly identify suspects and groups linked to terrorism. These also freeze any existing assets and disable terrorists' ability to raise or move further funds.

Working partnerships

The government works closely with the intelligence law enforcement agencies on this issue, and will continue to do so. The financial and business sectors are key partners in denying terrorists access to the UK's financial systems and products.

Charities and voluntary organisations play an important role in ensuring that funds they collect are not diverted to terrorist front organisations. The UK has played a key role in the production of a draft code of conduct for NGOs by the European Commission.

Preventing extremism

Following the attacks in London in July 2005, seven community-led working groups were set up under the banner of 'Preventing Extremism Together' (PET) to develop practical recommendations for tackling violent extremism.

To secure local input into these recommendations, Ministers visited nine towns and cities with large Muslim populations to discuss how government could work in partnership with them to prevent extremism.

1000 British Muslims took part in these consultations, and their comments were fed back into the community-led working groups.

Border security

All UK ports have a port policing strategy in place.

The port policing strategy will involve screening passengers and freight for illegal goods or equipment that could be used for terrorist activity. Freight will also be checked for signs of human trafficking.

The government has been strengthening the UK's border controls in recent years, and it now has extensive powers for counter-terrorist policing at ports.

On this issue, the Counter-Terrorism and Intelligence Directorate works closely with:
⇨ Immigration and Nationality Directorate
⇨ HM Revenue and Customs which has responsibility for border controls.

Radiation screening

Radiation screening equipment has now been introduced at ports and airports, and UK-bound goods vehicles and passengers are routinely screened for signs that they've carried or handled radioactive materials.

Surveillance

Surveillance is an indispensable way of gathering intelligence against terrorists and other sophisticated and ruthless criminals.

Surveillance means:
⇨ monitoring, observing and listening to individuals' movements, conversations and other activities or communications;
⇨ recording anything monitored, observed or listened to in the course of surveillance;
⇨ using a surveillance device.

Working with partners

The UK does not have one department that looks after all aspects of counter-terrorism.

Instead we take advantage of the expertise and resources of other departments, agencies, and wider organisations such as the emergency services and bring them together to work on specific aspects of delivering the counter-terrorism strategy.

The advantage is that departments, agencies and first responders maintain and benefit from their skills on a day-to-day basis but can also use this in a response to a terrorist incident.

⇨ The above information is reprinted with kind permission from the Home Office. Please visit www.homeoffice.gov.uk for more information.

© Crown copyright

FAQ about the terrorist threat

Information from the Government

Why won't you give out more detailed information about the nature of the threat or the Government's emergency plans?

We are committed to giving you as much information as we can about terrorism. Our guiding principle is that wherever we can give you information that will help to protect you, we will. But we also have a responsibility to protect people working in the intelligence and security fields, and not to give out information that could compromise their safety. This includes intelligence, which also needs to be carefully analysed and assessed, to work out whether it is reliable or not.

We know you understand that we will not go into the specific details of contingency plans, because if terrorists knew all the details of our preparations to respond to attacks, it would immediately make those plans vulnerable and put us at risk.

What is the current alert state? Is there a colour code?

We do not believe it is beneficial to the UK to have one single national system to indicate the current general level of threat. Rather than one blanket system, we operate specific systems in various public sectors and key industries, like aviation and the utilities. This reflects the fact that when alert states need to be raised in one sector, the threat assessment for other sectors could stay the same. Our concern is always to minimise the damage to the economy and our prosperity caused by alarms of this nature.

Information on the general level of threat must be meaningful if it is to be of practical use. We provide regular assessments of the threat, set in context, to the public and to Parliament.

Of course, if a warning, or specific advice, is ever necessary to protect public safety and save lives, we will issue it without hesitation. We have systems in place to put those immediate warnings out if necessary.

What should I do if there is a terrorist attack?

If you are at the site of an incident, follow the instructions of the emergency services.

There is no such thing as a standard chemical or biological incident, and therefore no such thing as a standard response

---

If it is a major incident, and you are not in the immediate area, our advice is to 'go in, stay in, tune in'. Go home or go inside some other safe location, stay indoors and tune in to local radio or television news programmes for advice and information. We will issue advice immediately, through all forms necessary, if you need to take specific action.

It is always sensible to have a battery-powered or wind-up radio in the house to prepare for a range of emergencies, including power cuts and floods.

Do I need to buy a gas mask or protective suit to protect myself from chemical or biological threats? And do I need to stockpile food, water, or anything else?

No. There is currently no information that would lead us to advise you to obtain protective clothing, including gas masks, or to take other special precautions. However, it is always sensible to be prepared for a range of emergencies, including severe weather or floods. We will

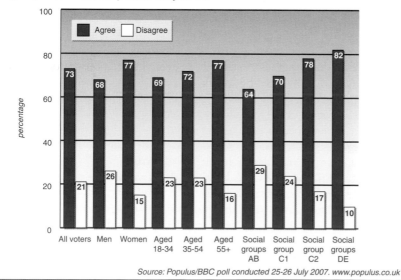

Police detention of terror suspects

This month (July 2007) Gordon Brown has been outlining new counter-terrorism measures, including a new unified border force, and allowing police to detain terror suspects for longer than the current maximum of 28 days. Please say whether you agree or disagree with the following statement.

Government should put combating terrorism ahead of concerns for civil liberties, and give police whatever powers they need.

Legend: ■ Agree □ Disagree

	Agree	Disagree
All voters	73	21
Men	68	26
Women	77	15
Aged 18-34	69	23
Aged 35-54	72	23
Aged 55+	77	16
Social groups AB	64	29
Social group C1	70	24
Social group C2	78	17
Social groups DE	82	10

Source: Populus/BBC poll conducted 25-26 July 2007. www.populus.co.uk

issue advice immediately if you need to take specific action.

How will I know what to do if there is a chemical or biological incident? And why can't you tell us more in advance?

There is no such thing as a standard chemical or biological incident, and therefore no such thing as a standard response.

___

The UK aviation security regime is one of the most developed in the world

___

How we respond to a chemical or biological incident – accidental or otherwise – would depend on a number of factors. The emergency services are best placed to decide the appropriate response, taking into account the relevant factors.

To give detailed advice in advance about how to handle every potential threat would be misleading and unhelpful. Worse, it could lead to confusion in an actual incident – the advice given for one type of situation might be wrong in different circumstances.

We, and the emergency services, will provide immediate information and advice in the event of a discernible threat or a specific incident.

At the moment, we do not believe that the best way to offer useful, up-to-date advice is to issue a national leaflet.

There has been a lot of media coverage about people getting smallpox vaccinations. Do I need a vaccination and can I get one from my GP?

No. Smallpox was declared eradicated in 1980. Consequently, smallpox vaccinations are not available on the NHS through family doctors and General Practitioners do not hold stocks of the vaccine.

The Department of Health holds a strategic stock for use in an emergency, which can and will be distributed quickly in the event of a bio-terrorism incident involving smallpox, but they are not currently recommending vaccination for the wider UK public. This decision follows World Health Organisation guidelines about how best to protect the public. It has not been taken lightly, and the situation is being kept under very careful review.

The Department of Health have recommended vaccination for a small number of frontline health-service staff and military personnel. This is because these frontline staff and personnel would provide the first response if there were a confirmed, suspected or threatened release of smallpox.

Contingency plans for dealing with smallpox are detailed in the draft guidelines on smallpox available on the Department of Health website.

Is it safe to visit and travel around London?

London has lived with the threat of terrorism for more than 30 years. Operational responses are well co-ordinated, regularly practised and continually reviewed.

Since the September 11 attacks in the US, additional measures have been taken, including specific counter-terrorism funding to the Metropolitan Police and detailed work by London Underground with the emergency services and security services to ensure systems are in place to deter or deal with an attack.

Strategic emergency planning for the Capital is lead by the London Resilience Forum (LRF). The LRF considers all aspects of the threat against the Capital and has contingency plans in place, which are regularly exercised.

The LRF is chaired by Nick Raynsford as Minister for London Resilience, with the Mayor as his deputy, and comprises the heads of the emergency services and London Underground, plus senior-level representatives from the city's local authorities and utilities, as well as the Home Office and the Cabinet Office.

Is there anyone I should be looking out for specifically?

It is their actions that give terrorists away, not their appearances. While you should stay alert to suspicious behaviour, it is very important to remember that terrorism affects us all. No community or religion should be made a scapegoat for the actions of terrorists. People of many faiths died on September 11, and the leaders of all faiths condemned the attacks.

We have a clear vision of a multi-cultural Britain – one that values the contribution made by each of our many ethnic, cultural and faith communities.

We are determined to see a truly dynamic society, in which people from different backgrounds can live and work together – whilst retaining their distinctive identities – in an atmosphere of mutual respect and understanding.

If you see harassment or discrimination, do not ignore it. It is everyone's responsibility to prevent it.

What if there is a terrorist attack and my children are at school?

In the event of a specific terrorist threat or incident, the local police will work with schools to ensure they are protected and to enact their emergency plans as necessary. The action taken would depend on the incident itself, and would not be very different from the emergency plans that schools already have for fire evacuations and bomb threats.

All schools and Local Education Authorities in England have been made aware that they can access guidance on dealing with terrorism via the UK Resilience website. Many local authorities have also issued guidance to schools in their area to assist in emergency planning.

Is it safe to fly?

The UK aviation security regime is one of the most developed in the world. It was further tightened in the aftermath of the September 11 attacks in the United States. The programme is kept under permanent review and adjusted when necessary.

Our aviation security programme works on many levels, with measures for all stages of the process – from check-in through to the flight itself. Not all of the measures are obvious: a lot goes on behind the scenes.

In May 2002 the Home Office and the Department for Transport appointed Sir John Wheeler to carry out a major independent review of airport security and policing. With the Department for Transport, we accepted and are now implementing the additional measures recommended in his October 2002 report.

Security measures on the ground currently include an enhanced passenger searching regime, and a tightening up of the articles that cannot be taken into an aircraft cabin.

Amongst in-flight security measures are regulations ensuring that cockpit doors on all aircraft leaving the UK and using UK airspace are locked. We are also implementing a requirement to fit strengthened cockpit doors, six months ahead of the international deadline.

It is their actions that give terrorists away, not their appearances. While you should stay alert to suspicious behaviour, it is very important to remember that terrorism affects us all

---

In 2002, we also decided to reinforce the existing package of measures for in-flight security by developing a capability to place covert, specially trained armed police officers aboard UK civil aircraft, should that be warranted.

What about my pets or animals?

The handling of animals, including pets, would depend very much on the particular circumstances of an incident. In drawing up contingency plans following the deliberate release of biological agents, such as infectious diseases, we have given consideration to the handling of animals.

Should businesses purchase their own equipment to detect chemical, biological or radiological materials as part of their counter-terrorism contingency plans?

No. We take contingency planning for potential terrorist attack very seriously and are working with the emergency services to ensure that they have the equipment they need to protect the public from the use of chemical, biological or radiological (CBR) materials. Effective measures are in place to detect such substances on a routine basis, where required, and equipment is regularly tested by independent scientists and other relevant agencies, including the emergency services.

The demanding and potentially dangerous job of detecting such materials should therefore be left to personnel in the emergency services and responsible agencies who are professionally trained in the necessary equipment. Businesses considering measures to prevent or reduce the impact of terrorism should contact the counter-terrorist security adviser in their local police force who will be able to give further advice.

Is it true that it is easy for potential terrorists to obtain dangerous chemicals and dirty bomb ingredients in the UK?

No, this is not true.
Updated 23 March 2007

⇨ Reprinted with kind permission from the Government and also Harlow Council, who are responsible for collating this information. Visit www.direct.gov.uk for more.

© *Crown copyright*

Major increase in work to tackle violent extremism

Information from BritainUSA

Communities Secretary Hazel Blears announced a major acceleration in government work to support communities to confront and isolate violent extremism.

In her first major speech on tackling violent extremism, Secretary Blears addressed 500 key opinion formers – from local government, police, academia and the third sector – and set out the challenge we face, how it is evolving and how it can be tackled.

She noted that extremists' messages are gaining most traction among young men (overwhelmingly between 16- to 35-year-olds) – with teenagers making up a significant proportion of the small minority that are drawn into extremism.

Extremists' operating methods and use of technology are becoming ever more sophisticated. They are exploiting ungoverned spaces such as the internet, bookshops, gyms and cafes and using new media to put across slick and seductive messages. The government's strategy will gear up and adapt to the evolving nature of the challenge.

Tackling violent extremism must be a shared endeavour where central and local government, police, voluntary organisations and communities themselves need to be bolder in tackling this issue. People must be equipped with the skills and strength to withstand the messages of extremists preaching division and hatred.

Hazel Blears announced that the department will invest £70 million ($144 million) in stepping up work to build resilience to violent extremism.

The Department will invest around £25 million ($51 million) in national schemes to support communities directly including:
⇨ Equipping faith leaders with the skills and understanding required to lead communities, building their capacity to engage with young people on the challenges they face, including extremism. For example, ensuring imams can communicate more effectively with young people;

Extremists' operating methods and use of technology are becoming ever more sophisticated

⇨ Supporting communities to broaden the provision of citizenship education in mosque schools, equipping young people themselves with the understanding and arguments to reject extremists' messages;
⇨ Developing new minimum standards for public institutions (e.g. prisons, universities) engaging imams working with young or vulnerable people;
⇨ Supporting the Charity Commission's work to improve governance standards in faith institutions, including mosques;
⇨ Increasing the provision of leadership training available to Muslim communities, particularly women and young people.

In addition there will be a step-change in the support available to local authorities with their community partners. £45 million ($93 million) will be available over the next three years – doubling existing funding levels by 08/09 and tripling them by 10/11. This will enable a broadening and deepening of work already under way across 70 local authority areas.

Secretary Blears set out her priorities for this going forward. These include:
⇨ a greater focus on teenagers and young people building their resilience to extremists' messages and giving them the strength and skills to face down the voices of division in later life;
⇨ more projects that reach out to young people (16- to 35-year-olds) – particularly the disaffected – such as mentoring or peer-support programmes;
⇨ Internet-based projects to provide platforms for engaging young Muslims and fostering tolerance and understanding;
⇨ more work to support and empower grassroots communities to play a leading role. This includes a major expansion in the work with Muslim women and young people, building their capacity to shape their communities and to engage with disaffected groups.

A lot of work is already being done by the Muslim communities in these areas and government will focus on supporting and accelerating that work.

Secretary Blears said:

'Given the scale and enduring nature of the threat we face, tough security measures are vital. But they cannot be the whole solution. We have to overcome this challenge by giving communities the strength and skills to face down a false and perverted ideology. This struggle will be with us for years to come, and we must do more to support the next generation in winning it. That is why we will be putting work with young people and Muslim women centre-stage, giving the silent majority a voice.'

Background

The government will support communities delivering projects in a number of areas. This will be a community-led approach building on excellent work already under way.

Children and young people

The government needs to ensure that children and young people – particularly in their formative years – are equipped with the skills and confidence to reject extremist messages. Mainstream schools and mosque schools have a key role to play in supporting this.

Many mosque schools – like those in Bradford – are working to make citizenship education a key pillar of their curriculum. Citizenship teaching combined with a greater understanding of the faith are a key aspect of ensuring young Muslims are resilient to extremist messages.

Role models/mentors

A lack of inspirational role models can be a factor in young people becoming vulnerable to extremist messages. That's why we will support more mentoring projects that reach out to those that are vulnerable and disaffected using successful local business leaders, religious and youth leaders, and academics.

Funding will be used to increase work with voluntary groups already plugged into some of the hardest to reach Muslim youth who are also the most susceptible to radicalisation.

That includes working with, for example, excluded children who may be vulnerable to extremists.

Internet-based projects

The funding will facilitate an expansion of Internet-based projects, radio stations and webcasts which are locally run and managed to give young people spaces and forums to share their views and discuss issues such as democracy and shared values. By encouraging young people to discuss these issues openly we will seek to undermine the influence of extremists who use the web as a propaganda tool to radicalise young British Muslims.

Working directly with Muslim communities

Extremists distort the true nature of Islam to justify their hatred and violence. Study circles, citizenship teaching, seminars and workshops run by youth leaders and Islamic scholars will help young people to develop a firmer grounding in Islam and rebut the arguments of those who preach division and hatred. Alongside that the funding will enable a major expansion of leadership training for Muslim women and young people. This is likely to include training to enable communities to benefit from the skills and experience of community leaders, for example in the business community.

A new national network of Muslim women will be established to advise government and work with communities across the country. This will enable us to ensure that more women's voices are heard and develop a clearer view of what needs to be done to support Muslim women – e.g. developing leadership skills.

Supporting communities to drive up standards of governance in mosques

Strong mosques positioned at the centre of the community and effectively governed will be better placed to serve and enrich those communities. It will also leave them better placed to confront and isolate extremists' efforts to infiltrate their communities.

The Mosques and Imams National Advisory Board (MINAB) has launched a consultation on a framework of core minimum standards for mosques in the UK. This will help bring about improvements in governance, promote stronger leadership and communication skills for imams, strengthen financial management and develop mosques as centres of community cohesion and citizenship. MINAB will provide practical advice, guidance and support to Muslim communities.
31 October 2007

⇨ The above information is reprinted with kind permission from BritainUSA (the British Embassy). Visit www.britainusa.com for more information.

© *BritainUSA*

Racial profiling and anti-terror stop and search

Information from the Institute of Race Relations

Amid growing public concern about stop and search powers under terror laws and the challenge by Liberty in the High Court over their misuse, Arun Kundnani examines some of the key issues in the debate.

The new powers introduced under the Terrorism Act

Under the Police and Criminal Evidence Act (1984) stops could only be carried out by police if they had 'reasonable suspicion'. But in Section 44 of the Terrorism Act 2000 new powers were introduced to allow stops and searches in order to prevent terrorism – no such suspicion was required. To regulate the use of such wide powers a special process of ministerial authorisation was set up to restrict such stops to a limited place and time where it was thought, on the basis of specific intelligence, necessary to prevent terrorism. And before police forces could use these powers, an authorising officer of Association of Chief Police Officers (ACPO) rank had to issue an order with the reasons for the authorisation. The order could last no longer than 28 days and the Secretary of State had to approve the authorisation within 48 hours.

However, in practice, the Metropolitan police has had a rolling authorisation across its whole district since February 2001. This has been justified on the grounds that the whole of London has been under permanent threat of terrorist attack over this time. And this fact only emerged by chance. It was only during a court hearing into the policing of protests at an arms fair in the Docklands in October 2003 that it emerged that the Section 44 powers had, in fact, been renewed every 28 days since the Act came into force in

By Arun Kundnani

February 2001. Till then, the public had not even been told that these powers were in permanent effect.

The operation of these powers is surrounded with a climate of secrecy and non-accountability that cannot be justified by operational reasons alone.

> **The result of anti-terrorist stop and search is the criminalisation of entire communities and the placing of tens of thousands of innocent people under suspicion**

The Terrorism Act 2000 has led to 'racial profiling'

The so-called 'code A guidance' on Section 44 advises first that: 'Officers must take particular care not to discriminate against members of minority ethnic groups in the exercise of these powers.' But it goes on to say that: 'There may be circumstances, however, where it is appropriate for officers to take account of a person's ethnic origin in selecting persons to be stopped in response to a specific terrorist threat (for example, some international

terrorist groups are associated with particular ethnic identities). '[1] There is a concern that this clause effectively gives a licence to the police to stop and search people on the basis of an 'ethnic' profile of terrorist suspects, what US civil liberties activists would describe as 'racial profiling'.

Specifically, there is concern that police forces may be using Section 44 to target people who appear to police officers to be Muslim. The Home Office's *Stop & Search Action Team Interim Guidance*, which is a guidance document for police managers published in 2004, suggests this interpretation when it states that: 'There may be circumstances where it is appropriate for officers to take account of a person's ethnic background when they decide who to stop in response to a specific terrorist threat (for example, some international terrorist groups are associated with particular ethnic groups, such as Muslims). '[2] Of course, as the authors of this document ought to know, there is no such ethnic group as 'Muslims'. What is revealed here is anti-terrorism being used as a justification for racial profiling against Asians, Blacks and people of Middle Eastern

Since the terrorist attacks in 2005, London and other major cities have seen an increased police presence

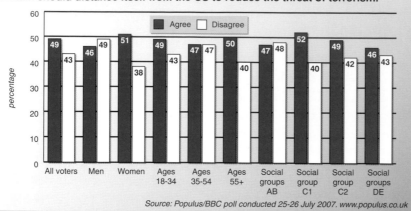

Britain's relationship with the United States

This month (July 2007) Gordon Brown has been outlining new counter-terrorism measures, including a new unified border force, and allowing police to detain terror suspects for longer than the current maximum of 28 days. Please say whether you agree or disagree with the following statement.

Britain should distance itself from the US to reduce the threat of terrorism.

Source: Populus/BBC poll conducted 25-26 July 2007. www.populus.co.uk

appearance – the ethnic groups police officers would most likely associate with Islam. This may explain why Blacks and Asians were both four times more likely than Whites to be stopped under these powers in 2002/03.[3] Furthermore, according to one recent report, the number of Asian and Black people stopped and searched in London streets by police using anti-terrorism powers increased more than twelvefold after the July 7 bombings. [4]

There seems to be confusion within the authorities as to whether such discriminatory stops are justifiable on this matter. In March 2005, Home Office minister Hazel Blears stated that Muslims should accept as 'reality' that they would be stopped and searched more often than others – going against the grain of much of the post-Macpherson agenda on stop and search.[5] On the other hand, documents such as the Association of Police Authorities' *Know your rights* leaflet, which is widely used as a guide for the public on their rights during a stop and search, states that: 'You should not be stopped or searched just because of: your age, race, gender, sexual orientation, disability, religion or faith; the way you look or dress, the language you speak.'[6] Two different messages are being sent out here. It is likely that Hazel Blears' message is a truer reflection of actual policing practices.

Stops found no terrorists

In the year 2002/3, police in England and Wales stopped and searched an average of 60 people a day as suspected terrorists, the majority while driving. That amounted to 21,577 stops and searches in one year under Terrorism Act powers. Whereas 13 per cent of stops and searches under normal police powers resulted in an arrest, the arrest rate for stops and searches on suspicion of terrorism was just 1.7 per cent. And the overwhelming majority of these arrests had nothing to do with terrorism. Only eighteen arrests in connection with terrorism were made in that year as a result of the 21,577 stops and searches carried out. None of these arrests resulted in a conviction for terrorist offences. [7] In other words, although tens of thousands of people were stopped and searched under suspicion of terrorism, these searches did not lead to a single conviction. The figures recorded in the following year showed a similar pattern. [8] By 2004/5 when one hundred people were stopped each day, 455 arrests were made out of 35,776 searches, a rate of 1.2 per cent. [9]

Can the powers be justified as a deterrent?

Police forces themselves know that they cannot justify anti-terrorist stops and searches in terms of convictions. That is why they now say that the real value of anti-terrorist stop and search is as a deterrent to would-be terrorists. Police authorities have given evidence in parliament that a terrorist who is planning to attack Westminster tube station, for example, may be deterred if he sees that he may be stopped and searched by police officers. [10]

Blacks and Asians were both four times more likely than Whites to be stopped under [stop and search] powers in 2002/03

But these powers were never justified to parliament on the basis of a general deterrent effect resulting from searches of people. The intention was that their use would be tied to specific intelligence and used with a view to disrupting and arresting terrorists. Furthermore, any plausible deterrent effect would require a reasonable likelihood that any terrorist would be stopped and searched in the midst of carrying out a terrorist operation. That would require such a massive use of stop and search powers as to severely disrupt the daily lives of millions of people in London, especially if, as the Metropolitan Police argue, there is a permanent London-wide threat of terrorist attack. To swamp the capital with such a large degree of arbitrary stops and searches that terrorists are likely to be deterred from attacking London is not only a huge waste of police resources which could be used more efficiently in preventing terrorism; it is also a hugely disproportionate price to pay in terms of particular communities' civil rights. Finally, it is hardly credible that terrorists will just give up a planned attack if they think that they might be searched by a police officer.

Criminalising communities

The result of anti-terrorist stop and search is the criminalisation of entire communities and the placing of tens of thousands of innocent people under suspicion. None of the lessons of the past – in relation to policing Black and Irish communities – appear to have been learnt. The damage to community relations is already clear. Youth workers in areas of London where police are targeting large numbers of Asian youths for stops and searches, such as in Tower Hamlets, describe an increasing atmosphere of tension. One youth worker reported that the situation locally was, in his words, like 'cowboys and Indians'. Even before 7/7, there were numerous anecdotes of young Asian men being stopped and searched, getting abused, being accused of membership of al-Qaida or even being beaten up. In many communities, there is a growing climate of fear; underground stations and bus stops have become places where police and immigration officers stop everyone whose skin colour or accent marks them out as suspect.

No redress

Though the Independent Police Complaints Commission can take up complaints about the manner in which Section 44 stops and searches are carried out, there appears to be no provision for complaints about the fact that the stop and search was carried out at all, even though this is the main cause of public concern. Complaining, as commonly happens, that a police officer carried out a stop and search without any reason is redundant when there is no requirement in the guidelines that there be 'reasonable grounds for suspicion'.

Misused on legitimate protesters

When the Terrorism Act 2000 was presented to parliament, it was argued that its measures were essential to meet the threat of international Islamic terrorism. Yet its powers are being used today against people who are protesting peacefully against the government. The very loose definition of terrorism in the 2000 Act leads to a real danger of Section 44 stop and search powers being used to suppress political dissent. Section 44 was used to search protesters outside the DSEi Arms Fair at the Excel Centre in Docklands in October 2003 and against anti-war protesters on their way to the Fairford Air Base earlier in 2003. It appears that stop and search was used on both these occasions for no other reason than to intimidate legitimate protesters. One protester at the Fairford military base, for example, was reportedly ordered by police to strip down to his vest and wait in the cold for twenty minutes during a search at night when the temperature had fallen to minus four degrees.

The new powers should be repealed

There is no evidence that Section 44 has helped prevent, detect or prosecute terrorism in any form and therefore new provisions should be repealed. For, if police officers have a reasonable suspicion that a criminal act, including terrorism, is about to be committed, they can in any event stop and search under the old PACE powers and go on to arrest a suspect if there are reasonable grounds.

Footnotes

1 *Police and Criminal Evidence Act 1984 Code A: Exercise by police officers of statutory powers of stop and search*, pp8-9.
2 Home Office, *Stop & Search Action Team, Interim Guidance*, 2004, p12.
3 *Section 95 Statistics on Race and the Criminal Justice System – 2003*, Home Office, 2004.
4 Vikram Dodd, 'Surge in stop and search of Asian people after July 7', *Guardian*, 24 December 2005.
5 Vikram Dodd and Alan Travis, 'Muslims face increased stop and search', *Guardian*, 2 March 2005.
6 Association of Police Authorities, *Stop and Search: know your rights*, April 2005.
7 Arun Kundnani, 'Analysis: the war on terror leads to racial profiling', *IRR News*, 7 July 2004.
8 *Section 95 Statistics on Race and the Criminal Justice System – 2004*, Home Office, 2005.
9 Ben Russell, 'Police stop and search 100 people a day under new anti-terror laws', *Independent*, 25 January 2006.
10 Oral evidence by Sir John Quinton, Metropolitan Police Authority, to House of Commons Home Affairs Committee, 8 July 2004.

31 January 2006

⇨ The above information is reprinted with kind permission from the Institute of Race Relations, a London-based think tank on the struggle for racial justice in the UK, Europe and around the world. Visit www.irr.org.uk for more information.

© IRR

A humane way to fight terrorism

Amnesty International's UK director, Kate Allen, explains why she believes the British Government is beginning to rethink the way it deals with the threat of terrorism

The Government has been getting it wrong on terrorism. It shouldn't have said that the 'rules of the game' were changing after the 2005 London bombings.

It shouldn't have bought into the grandiose concept of a 'war on terror', and it shouldn't have acted as if new laws were the answer to people armed with extremist views and home-made bombs.

This happens to be exactly what I believe, but interestingly enough these views were expressed just two weeks ago by the Government's Police and Security Minister Tony McNulty, speaking at the Labour Party Conference.

Coupled with similarly sensible, thoughtful remarks from Gordon Brown and the Home Secretary Jacqui Smith, this could signal a re-think. It's early days, and a draconian move to hold people for up to 56 days without charge is still on the cards, but my hope is that the Government has rethought the war on terror.

If Mr Brown's government – or indeed David Cameron's – can reaffirm the importance of proper policing and fair trials, it will put our lives and liberty on a surer footing and avoid some of the bear-traps that would otherwise hand the bombers a set of easy victories.

Why do I say this? Well, as the director of a human rights organisation rooted in nearly 50 years of defending core values like freedom, fairness and equality, I believe the world has been here before and, essentially, the world has made the same mistakes before as well.

The mistakes I have in mind are when governments rush through draconian laws or allow dirty counter-terrorism practices like torture and secret killings in the name of 'getting tough on terrorism'.

First of all, it rarely works. From the Black and Tans in Ireland in the 1920s, through the treatment of the Mau Mau in Kenya in the fifties, to the internment of mostly IRA suspects in Northern Ireland in the 1970s, heavy-handedness has rebounded.

Bedrock laws have been tampered with and Britain's reputation for fairness and the rule of law has been severely tarnished

---

It has generated new levels of resentment in local and minority communities. And it's led to a sudden and dangerous erosion of cherished values.

Bedrock laws have been tampered with and Britain's reputation for fairness and the rule of law has been severely tarnished.

Ultimately though, this approach has failed. Then, usually under new governments, repressive laws have been rolled back, tactics abandoned as a shameful error and new safeguards introduced.

In the past 50 years governments in countries as varied as Sri Lanka, Turkey, Algeria, Pakistan, Egypt, Russia/Chechnya, Nepal, China, Colombia and apartheid South Africa have all seen variations on a theme.

'Strike hard' or 'Get tough' policies have meant draconian measures, 'states of emergency', midnight round-ups and, sooner or later, torture in secret prisons and police station basements.

Yes, the levels of provocation can be extremely high. The pub bombings in Birmingham in 1974 were one of the worst moments in this country's recent history, leaving 21 people dead and over 180 injured. It was an appalling atrocity – surpassed in England only by the carnage of 7/7 – but it also led to a deeply regrettable reaction.

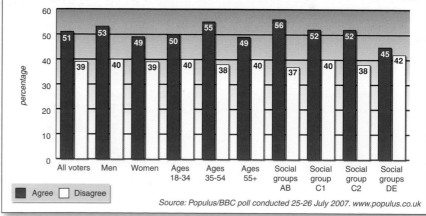

Anti-terror legislation

This month (July 2007) Gordon Brown has been outlining new counter-terrorism measures, including a new unified border force, and allowing police to detain terror suspects for longer than the current maximum of 28 days. Please say whether you agree or disagree with the following statement.

New laws will not make any difference to the level of terrorist threat Britain faces.

	Agree	Disagree
All voters	51	39
Men	53	40
Women	49	39
Ages 18-34	50	40
Ages 35-54	55	38
Ages 55+	49	40
Social groups AB	56	37
Social group C1	52	40
Social group C2	52	38
Social groups DE	45	42

Source: Populus/BBC poll conducted 25-26 July 2007. www.populus.co.uk

Six innocent men had false confessions beaten out of them and went on to spend 16 years in prison for a crime they didn't commit. It was a lamentable miscarriage of justice and one that badly damaged Britain's reputation.

Terrorism is vile and needs to be prevented. Where terrorists commit atrocities they need to be apprehended and punished with the full vigour of the law. Full stop. Let's make no bones about it, those that go out on to the streets of Madrid, Bali, or London to indiscriminately kill ordinary people are vicious criminals.

Knowing they can rarely if ever win on the 'battlefield', terrorists strive to generate fear and over-reaction

---

They clearly show by their actions that they are implacably opposed to tolerance, the law and human rights. It's bitterly regrettable that impressionable young people are impressed by their blood-curdling but nonsensical rhetoric.

But to overreact is a mistake. In fact it's one of the worst mistakes we can make. Knowing they can rarely if ever win on the 'battlefield', terrorists strive to generate fear and over-reaction.

Yes, such people are extremely dangerous, and yes they can use 'asymmetrical' tactics – the suicide bomber – to commit terrible atrocities. But we have seen their like before and we know how to deal with them.

Surveillance, policing, proper prosecution and imprisonment are the answers.

Richard Reid, the British-born 'shoe bomber' who intended to bring down a transatlantic jet flying between Paris and Miami, was tried in an ordinary US federal court and given a life sentence.

Zacarias Moussaoui, the 9/11 plotter, was tried and imprisoned for life. Likewise, the 'American Taliban' John Walker Lindh was convicted and is serving 20 years.

These prosecutions took place in the US, where the American Constitution values of liberty and law have had such an influence.

However, when, nearly six years ago, former US Defence Secretary Donald Rumsfeld and others set up the US military prison camp at Guantanamo, they departed from mainstream American legal values as well as long-established international human rights standards.

Murderous actions by armed groups the world over represent a pure abnegation of human rights. Their actions are essentially about goading and baiting us. They are waiting for the 'essential' new law that they will immediately feed straight back into their own propaganda. We need to be smarter than this. It's al Qaida and the so-called 'war on terrorism' today, but in one form or another this has been going on for decades.

Fighting groups who exploit 'terrorist' tactics – the PKK, FARC, the IRA, the Baader-Meinhof Gang, the Red Brigades, the PLO, the Tamil Tigers, al Qaida – has and must mean defending the values that differentiate us from organised kidnappers and killers in the first place.

If we surrender some of the cornerstones of national and international law, then we effectively surrender to those who were always hostile to human rights in the first place. Put simply, we must not undermine our own values in trying to defend them.

Today Amnesty International is launching a new campaign to unite people in opposition to human rights abuses in the 'war on terror'.

We are implacably opposed to terrorism, but we believe passionately in fundamental values – safety from torture, fair and equal treatment before the law.

We are bringing together a huge grass-roots movement of people who want to 'unsubscribe' from torture and secret detention as the supposed 'answers' to terrorism. Take a stand. Join us. Unsubscribe.

For more information, including how to take action in support of human rights in the 'war on terror', visit www. unsubscribe-me.org
9 October 2007

⇨ The above information is reprinted with kind permission from Amnesty International and was published in the *Birmingham Post*. Visit www.amnesty.org.uk for more.
© *Amnesty International*

⇨ The word 'terrorism' was coined during France's Reign of Terror in 1793-94. (page 1)

⇨ Most terrorists eschew the terrorist label, preferring to perceive themselves as irregular military forces [e.g. Irish Republican Army (IRA), Revolutionary Armed Forces of Colombia (FARC), Symbionese Liberation Army (SLA), etc.] (page 1)

⇨ As a result of modern transportation, communication and access to resources, terrorism is becoming an ever-increasing threat. Terrorists are not recognised as belonging to any army and seek to weaken or supplant existing political landscapes for political, nationalist or religious goals using violence and intimidation. (page 2)

⇨ MI5 investigates threats to the UK by gathering, analysing and assessing intelligence. 87% of MI5 resources work on counter-terrorism and protective security. (page 2)

⇨ Violent acts on behalf of political change are as old as human history. For example, the Sicarii were a first-century Jewish group who murdered enemies and collaborators in their campaign to oust their Roman rulers from Judea. (page 4)

⇨ International terrorism is considered to have gotten its start at the 1972 Munich Olympics, at which a Palestinian organisation, Black September, kidnapped and killed Israeli athletes preparing to compete. (page 4)

⇨ Muhammad Atta, the architect of the 9/11 attacks, and 'the Egyptian hijacker who was driving the first plane, was a near alcoholic and was drinking vodka before he boarded the aircraft'. Alcohol would be strictly off limits for a highly observant Muslim. Atta, and perhaps many others, are not simply orthodox believers turned violent, but rather violent extremists who manipulate religious concepts for their own purposes. (page 5)

⇨ 51% of people surveyed by Ipsos MORI in July 2005 felt that it was very likely London would experience another terrorist attack in the near future, compared to 43% surveyed in September 2005. (page 6)

⇨ 51% of people surveyed by Ipsos MORI in the September following the London bombings of 7 July 2005 felt that it was unacceptable to allow the police to have a 'shoot to kill' policy for suspected terrorists. 45% felt that it was acceptable. (page 7)

⇨ The Internet is a powerful tool for terrorists, who use online message boards and chat rooms to share information, coordinate attacks, spread propaganda, raise funds, and recruit, experts say. (page 8)

⇨ 13% of Muslims in the 16 to 24 age bracket claimed to admire organisations like Al-Qaeda that are prepared to fight against the West according to a Policy Exchange survey, compared to only 2% in the 45 to 54 age bracket. (page 11)

⇨ 70% of people taking part in a global issues survey by the Mental Health Foundation named terrorism as their biggest worry, ahead of immigration, climate change, natural disasters and the spread of nuclear weapons. (page 12)

⇨ Many students from 'hot spots' of Muslim unrest around the world are thought to obtain visas for study but 'go under the wire' by failing to show up for their courses when they arrive in Britain. (page 13)

⇨ The actions of an individual or a small group do not necessarily represent the beliefs of a particular religion nor its many adherents, and the religion itself cannot be held responsible for such actions. In reality, Islam not only condemns terrorism and suicide missions, but also prohibits them completely. (page 15)

⇨ Despite ongoing issues relating to the 2005 London bombings, the threat of terrorism and the impact of new immigrants to the country, people's own experiences of prejudice and discrimination appear relatively unchanged from previous years. (page 19)

⇨ Extremist behaviour by animal rights protesters has had the effect of increasing public support for testing new medical treatments on animals, a poll for the *Daily Telegraph* has found. (page 20)

⇨ 77% of people surveyed by YouGov felt that it was fair to describe animal rights activists engaging in extreme acts such as death threats, planting bombs and digging up human remains for the purposes of intimidation as 'terrorists'. (page 25)

⇨ In a Theos survey, the youngest class of respondents (18-25) were more than twice as likely as those over 65 to regard Islam as 'fundamentally a religion of war'. (page 27)

⇨ 73% of UK voters agreed that the government should put combating terrorism ahead of concerns for civil liberties, and give police whatever powers they need. 21% did not agree, according to a Populus poll. (page 30)

⇨ 49% of UK voters agreed that Britain should distance itself from the US to reduce the threat of terrorism. 43% did not agree, according to a Populus poll. (page 36)

GLOSSARY

The 7/7 bombings

Said as *seven seven* (after the fashion of the US 9/11) and also know as the London bombings, this refers to the events of 7 July 2005, the date on which four suicide bombers caused the deaths of 56 people on the London transport system. The incident was the deadliest single act of terrorism in the UK since Lockerbie (the 1988 bombing of Pan Am Flight 103 which killed 270), and the deadliest bombing in London since the Second World War. The attacks were significant in drawing UK attention to the terrorism problem – they demonstrated that terrorism could occur at home as well as abroad, and could even be perpetrated by British citizens (three of the four bombers were born and raised in the UK).

9/11

9/11 (said as *nine eleven*) is a common way of referring to the events of 11 September 2001, the date on which four passenger planes were hijacked by Islamic militants and flown into US targets – notably the twin towers of the World Trade Centre in New York, and also the Pentagon building – causing thousands of lives to be lost. These attacks were significant in bringing terrorism into the international spotlight, changing the world's political climate and launching the 'War on Terror'.

Animal rights activism

Animal rights activists object to the exploitation of animals by human beings, and in recent years their particular focus has been the use of animals in medical tests by pharmaceutical companies. Extremists have been known to use tactics including death threats, planting bombs and destroying property against pharmaceutical workers and their families, and there is a debate as to whether these activists should also be described as terrorists.

Counter-terrorism

Counter-terrorism refers to the tactics and techniques used by governments and other groups to prevent or minimise a terrorist threat.

Cyberterrorism

A term coined to describe the increasing use of the Internet as a vehicle through which terrorists can launch an attack. Terrorists could conceivably hack into electrical grids and security systems, or perhaps distribute a powerful computer virus.

Detention without charge

The Terrorism Act 2006, the most recent piece of anti-terror legislation, introduced several new counter-terrorism measures, most controversially granting the police the power to detain terror suspects for up to 28 days without charge (previously 14 days had been the maximum). Some feel that this period is too long to detain someone without charge and infringes on their civil liberties, whereas others feel it is not long enough and prevents the police from doing their job effectively – originally, the detention period proposed was 90 days, and critics including the police and government ministers continue to lobby for an extension to the 28-day period.

Extremism

Extremism refers to beliefs or practices that are considered beyond the norm or radical. Extremism can give rise to militance, and in the context of terrorism is often thought of in connection with religion – religious terrorism is considered the most alarming terrorist threat at work today. Groups justifying their violence on Islamic grounds, such as Al Qaeda or Hamas, often come to mind first, but Christianity, Judaism and Hinduism have all given rise to their own forms of militant extremism.

Jihad

The concept of *Jihad* is fundamental to the Islamic religion, but is often misinterpreted by the media as meaning only a 'holy war'. In fact, *Jihad* refers to self-purification and derives from the term to strive, struggle, exert oneself and to be willing to overcome evil for good.

Security

Security is the state of being or feeling secure. In the context of discussions about terrorism, it refers to the safety of a country and its people against criminal activities perpetrated by terrorist groups or individuals.

Stop and search

Police received extended powers to stop and search individuals in order to prevent terrorism in the Terrorism Act 2000. There have been concerns that the new powers have led to 'racial profiling', whereby police are likely to stop and search people on the basis of an 'ethnic' profile of terrorist suspects. In the current climate, this is likely to mean those belonging to an ethnic group police are most likely to associate with Islam. Black and Asian people were four times more likely than white people to be stopped under these powers in 2002/03.

Terrorism

The word 'terrorism' dates back to the 18th century, but there is no globally accepted definition of the term. The most widely accepted is probably that put forward by the US State Department, which states that terrorism is 'premeditated, politically motivated violence perpetrated against non-combatant targets by subnational groups or clandestine agents, usually intended to influence an audience.' Types include Nationalist-Separatist, Religious, Right-Wing and Left-Wing Terrorism.

INDEX

Additional Resources

Other Issues titles

If you are interested in researching further some of the issues raised in *The Terrorism Problem*, you may like to read the following titles in the **Issues** series:

⇨ Vol. 150 *Migration and Population* (ISBN 978 1 86168 423 3)

⇨ Vol. 148 *Religious Beliefs* (ISBN 978 1 86168 421 9)

⇨ Vol. 142 *Media Issues* (ISBN 978 1 86168 408 0)

⇨ Vol. 137 *Crime and Anti-Social Behaviour* (ISBN 978 1 86168 389 2)

⇨ Vol. 131 *Citizenship and National Identity* (ISBN 978 1 86168 377 9)

⇨ Vol. 121 *The Censorship Debate* (ISBN 978 1 86168 354 0)

⇨ Vol. 120 *The Human Rights Issue* (ISBN 978 1 86168 353 3)

⇨ Vol. 116 *Grief and Loss* (ISBN 978 1 86168 349 6)

⇨ Vol. 115 *Racial Discrimination* (ISBN 978 1 86168 348 9)

⇨ Vol. 104 *Our Internet Society* (ISBN 978 1 86168 324 3)

⇨ Vol. 89 *Refugees* (ISBN 978 1 86168 290 1)

⇨ Vol. 82 *Protecting our Privacy* (ISBN 978 1 86168 277 2)

For more information about these titles, visit our website at www.independence.co.uk/publicationslist

Useful organisations

You may find the websites of the following organisations useful for further research:

⇨ **About.com:** www.about.com

⇨ **Amnesty International:** www.amnesty.org.uk

⇨ **BritainUSA:** www.britainusa.com

⇨ **Council on Foreign Relations:** www.cfr.org

⇨ **Economic and Social Research Council:** www.esrc.ac.uk

⇨ **Forum Against Islamophobia and Racism:** www.fairuk.org

⇨ **The Home Office:** www.homeoffice.gov.uk

⇨ **Institute of Race Relations:** www.irr.org.uk

⇨ **Ipsos MORI:** www.ipsos-mori.com

⇨ **Policy Exchange:** www.policyexchange.org.uk

⇨ **Spiked:** www.spiked-online.com

⇨ **Theos:** www.theosthinktank.co.uk

⇨ **Unsubscribe:** www.unsubscribe-me.org

⇨ **US Foreign Policy Association:** www.fpa.org

⇨ **YouGov:** www.yougov.com

ACKNOWLEDGEMENTS

The publisher is grateful for permission to reproduce the following material.

While every care has been taken to trace and acknowledge copyright, the publisher tenders its apology for any accidental infringement or where copyright has proved untraceable. The publisher would be pleased to come to a suitable arrangement in any such case with the rightful owner.

Chapter One: Terrorism

Classifying terrorism, © Foreign Policy Association, *Security and terrorism in the UK,* © Economic and Social Research Council, *History of terrorism,* © About.com, *Timeline: terrorism threats to the UK,* © Guardian Newspapers Ltd, *Facts and figures,* © Crown copyright is reproduced with the permission of Her Majesty's Stationery Office, *Head of MI5: terror threat is growing,* © Crown copyright is reproduced with the permission of Her Majesty's Stationery Office, *Terrorists and the Internet,* © Council on Foreign Relations, *We are offering the terrorist a megaphone,* © Guardian Newspapers Ltd, *Fear of terrorism,* © Adfero Ltd, *New UK terror threat from foreign students,* © Telegraph Group Ltd, *Islam, terrorism and September 11,* © Forum Against Islamophobia and Racism, *Young, British Muslims getting more radical,* © Telegraph Group Ltd, *The hijacking of British Islam,* © Policy Exchange, *Race relations 2006,* © Ipsos MORI, *Public turns on animal terrorists,* © Telegraph Group Ltd, *Animal rights terrorism is on the increase,* © Daily Standard, *The truth about 'animal rights terrorism',* © Spiked.

Chapter Two: Tackling Terrorism

How do we counter terrorism?, © Theos, *Terrorism Act 2006,* © Crown copyright is reproduced with the permission of Her Majesty's Stationery Office, *Counter-terrorism strategy,* © Crown copyright is reproduced with the permission of Her Majesty's Stationery Office, *FAQ about the terrorist threat,* © Crown copyright is reproduced with the permission of Her Majesty's Stationery Office, *Major increase in work to tackle violent extremism,* © Crown copyright is reproduced with the permission of Her Majesty's Stationery Office, *Racial profiling and anti-terror stop and search,* © Institute of Race Relations, *A humane way to fight terrorism,* © Amnesty International.

Photographs

Flickr: pages 9 (kk+); 10 (Kimba Howard); 18 (Lucia H); 24 (James Jin); 35 (openDemocracy).
Stock Xchng: pages 14 (Benjamin Earwicker); 28 (drouu); 33 (Thomas Gray).
Wikimedia Commons: page 31 (Johan Elisson).

Illustrations

Pages 1, 32: Don Hatcher; pages 13, 34: Bev Aisbett; pages 26, 39: Angelo Madrid; pages 29, 37: Simon Kneebone.

Research by Sophie Crewdson, with additional research by Claire Owen and Lisa Firth on behalf of Independence Educational Publishers.

Additional editorial by Claire Owen on behalf of Independence Educational Publishers.

And with thanks to the team: Mary Chapman, Sandra Dennis, Claire Owen and Jan Sunderland.

Lisa Firth
Cambridge
January, 2008